KU-734-404

Frank Rudman

POEMS

FROM NEW WRITING

POEMS
FROM NEW WRITING
1936 - 1946

With a Foreword by

JOHN LEHMANN

JOHN LEHMANN
LONDON
1946

First published in 1946

MADE AND PRINTED IN GREAT BRITAIN BY PURNELL AND SONS, LTD.,
PAULTON (SOMERSET) AND LONDON

FOREWORD

THE first volume of *New Writing* was published in the Spring of 1936. It contained twenty contributions, and of those only two were poetry: a translation of Boris Pasternak's long poem *1905* by Alec Brown, and four poems by Stephen Spender, three of them translations from Hoelderlin.

One original poem in the first volume: the second contained none at all. But in the third volume W. H. Auden's *Lay Your Sleeping Head My Love* made its first appearance, together with original poems by Stephen Spender, Roy Fuller, Clifford Dyment, and poems translated from the Spanish and Polish. Ever since that time poetry played an important part in the volumes of *New Writing* as they came out every six months, and, later, in the more frequent issues of *Penguin New Writing*, which combined poems originally published in the big volumes with new poems. If anything the number of pages devoted to poetry increased during the war years: this was not, I think, due to deliberate policy, but to the fact that, at any rate among the authors who came within my scope, a far greater volume of poetry was being written than before.

The present anthology is an attempt to collect the best and most interesting poems which appeared under my editorship during those ten years,[1] whether in *New Writing*, *Folios of New Writing*, *New Writing & Daylight*, or *The Penguin New Writing*. I will not claim for it that every young poet of significance writing during the period is represented, for I am well aware that one or two names are absent which no one would leave out who was counting the stars of our time; but I do claim that it contains—and I was agreeably surprised to discover it as I made the choice—a high proportion of the outstanding poems that were written between the beginning of the Spanish Civil War and the end of the European War, perhaps higher than any other single editor can proudly stick as feathers in his cap.

The Spanish War is a gloomy milestone for creative writers, marking as it does the second descent of the twentieth century

---

[1] I have not included any poem which appeared later than *New Writing & Daylight 6* or *Penguin New Writing 26*.

into the violence of international anarchy, a descent made more destructive for them by the confusion of warring ideologies with warring empires. Rare and lucky were the poets who could find the calm and leisure in the midst of such events for continuous poetic creation at the deepest level ; and yet these events, by the passions they excited and the drama they manifested, involving the oldest beliefs and allegiances and spiritual hankerings of our civilization, were material that most young poets would find it difficult to refuse in any age. Our age, however, has been distinguished above all other ages by the tendency, in all fields of activity, to exploit whatever comes to hand as immediately and intensively as possible ; and poetry has not escaped the workings of this impulse, though prose fiction bears the deeper trace. An anthology could, of course, be made from the poetry of the last ten years in which topical disturbances were only present in the most indirect and remote way, and its quality would be high ; it would nevertheless exclude a great deal of equally high quality —I am not speaking of the abundant poetry which is little more than verse-journalism—which has had a more vivid meaning for the men and women who have lived and died among the wars and rumours of wars. It is this latter poetry in particular (though never exclusively), which *New Writing*, from the time I founded it, set itself to provide a medium for ; and that is why I believe that this anthology may turn out to be a peculiarly interesting poetic mirror of the history of our time. With this in mind I have kept the order of poems as far as possible to the chronological order of publication.

The poems in the first volume of *New Writing* were few, but they managed to be typical of what was to come in more than this emphasis on contemporary awareness : they included translations from other European literatures, and one of them was an unusually long poem. *New Writing* has consistently opened its pages to translations from French, Greek, Czech, Polish, Spanish and other languages ; and, equally consistently, to poems of a length rarely acceptable to the average weekly or monthly. The space it afforded as a book-magazine made this possible, and it eventually became a pioneer of the long poem—and the translated long poem—for many other book-magazines which followed it; so that one can say that a poet who runs to length has today as good a chance of being printed in periodicals as a poet who expresses himself more naturally in short lyrics.

In more than one way, therefore,—though for various reasons I have been able to include only a few of the longest poems—I hope that this anthology will have a flavour and *raison d'être* distinct from that of the many other anthologies which it is bound in some degree to overlap; quite apart from standing for judgment as a record of one man's taste and the encouragement he endeavoured to give to the making of poetry—to the building of dykes during the ten years of flood weather.

Thanks and acknowledgements are due to all the authors, their representatives, or their executors, and to the following publishers: Messrs. Allen and Unwin Ltd. for the poem by Alun Lewis (reprinted in *Ha! Ha! Among the Trumpets*); Messrs. Jonathan Cape Ltd. for poems by Cecil Day Lewis (*Word Over All*) and Henry Reed (*A Map of Verona*); Messrs. Cassell and Co. Ltd. for poems by Robert Graves (*Poems 1939–1945*); Messrs. Chatto and Windus for poems by Peter Yates (*The Motionless Dancer*); Messrs. Faber and Faber Ltd. for poems by W. H. Auden (*Another Time*), George Barker (*Eros in Dogma*), Norman Nicholson (*Five Rivers*), Anne Ridler (*Nine Bright Shiners*), Stephen Spender (*Trial of a Judge, Ruins and Visions, Poems of Dedication*); The Hogarth Press for poems by Roy Fuller (*The Middle of a War* and *A Lost Season*), Laurie Lee (*The Sun My Monument*), John Lehmann (*Forty Poems, The Sphere of Glass*), Terence Tiller (*Poems, The Inward Animal*); Messrs. Macmillan and Co. for poems by Edith Sitwell (*A Song of the Cold*); Poetry (London) Editions for poems by David Gascoyne (*Poems*); Messrs. George Routledge and Sons Ltd. for poems by Alex Comfort (*Elegies*) and John Heath-Stubbs (*The Divided Ways*).

JOHN LEHMANN.

CONTENTS

(arranged in alphabetical order of author's names)

[9]

[12]

[14]

THE SAD STANDARDS

ALAS for the sad standards
In the eyes of the old masters
Sprouting through glaze of their pictures!

For what we stare at through glass
Opens on to our running time:
As nature spilled before the summer mansion
Pours through windows in on our dimension:

And the propellor's rigid transparent flicker
To airman over continental ranges
Between him and the towns and river
Spells dynamics of this rotating
Age of invention, too rapid for sight.

Varnish over paint and dust across glass:
Stare back, remote, the static drum;
The locked ripeness of the centaur's feast;
The blowing flags, frozen stiff
In a cracked fog, and the facing
Reproach of Rembrandt's self-portrait.

Alas for the sad standards
In the eyes of freshly dead young
Sprawled in the mud of battle.
Stare back, stare back, with dust over glazed
Eyes, their gaze at partridges,
Their dreams of girls, and their collected
Faith in home, wound up like a little watch.

To ram them outside time, violence
Of wills that ride the cresting day
Struck them with lead so swift

Their falling sight stared through its glass.
Our sight stares back on death, like glass
Infringing the rigid eyes with toneless gaze,
Sinking stretched bodies inch-deep in their frames.

Through glass their eyes meet ours
Like standards of the masters
That shock us with their peace.

Stephen Spender.

LAY YOUR SLEEPING HEAD

LAY your sleeping head, my love,
Human on my faithless arm;
Time and fevers burn away
Individual beauty from
Thoughtful children, and the grave
Proves the child ephemeral:
But in my arms till break of day
Let the living creature lie,
Mortal, guilty, but to me
The entirely beautiful.

Soul and body have no bounds:
To lovers as they lie upon
Her tolerant enchanted slope
In their ordinary swoon,
Grave the vision Venus sends
Of supernatural sympathy,
Universal love and hope:
While an abstract insight wakes
Among the glaciers and the rocks
The hermit's sensual ecstasy.

[18]

Certainty, fidelity
On the stroke of midnight pass
Like vibrations of a bell,
And fashionable madmen raise
Their pedantic boring cry ;
Every farthing of the cost,
All the dreaded cards foretell
Shall be paid, but from this night
Not a whisper, not a thought,
Not a kiss nor look be lost.

Beauty, midnight, vision dies :
Let the winds of dawn that blow
Softly round your dreaming head
Such a day of sweetness show
Eye and knocking heart may bless,
Find the mortal world enough ;
Noons of dryness see you fed
By the involuntary powers,
Nights of insult let you pass
Watched by every human love.

W. H. Auden.

JUNE THUNDER

THE Junes were free and full, driving through tiny
Roads, the mudguards brushing the cow-parsley,
Through fields of mustard and under boldly embattled
        Mays and chestnuts.

Or between beeches verdurous and voluptuous
Or where broom and gorse beflagged the chalkland—
All the flare and gusto of the unenduring
        Joys of a season

[19]

Now returned but I note as more appropriate
To the maturer moods impending thunder
With an indigo sky and the garden hushed except for
           The treetops moving.

Then the curtains in my room blow suddenly inward
The shrubbery rustles, birds fly heavily homeward,
The white flowers fade to nothing on the trees and rain comes
           Down like a drop scene.

Now there comes the catharsis, the cleansing downpour
Breaking the blossoms of our overdated fancies,
Our old sentimentality and whimsicality,
           Loves of the morning.

Blackness at half-past eight, the night's precursor,
Clouds like falling masonry and lightning's lavish
Annunciation, the sword of the mad archangel
           Flashed from the scabbard.

If only you would come and dare the crystal
Rampart of rain and the bottomless moat of thunder
If only now you would come I should be happy
           Now if now only.

Louis MacNeice.

LODZ

My heart is heavy with songs and fears ;
Hide the fears in the heart and carry them,
Take up a song like a stone and hurl it
Where sulphurous smoke clouds drift over Lodz.

Cold in the morning whistle the sirens,
With tall clenched fists the chimneys menace ;
Our day, like a sore in rough red brickwork
Is filled with the iodine drops of night.
If once it would drown the day with its anger
Shafting of shops would turn no longer,
The soft white writhing coils would rest,
And death step out of the cotton bundles.

My heart is filled with smouldering fears,
Fires of the blood are banked but burning ;
With trail of smoke in the heavens a warning,
The song will fall like a spark upon Lodz.

Fire and blood react, give gold ;
Paper pulsates in secret places ;
Mills are roaring with turbulent labour
Fattening the owners at our expenses :
Joy for them, from our misery free,
For us, the hoofs of established order,
Yet far on horizon the storm approaches,
There will be thunder over the Republic.

My heart is heavy with will and power,
Light the spark and hurl it afar,
Breathe in the lungs the furious whirlwind
Tomorrow will waken another Lodz.

News will come like a torch from Warsaw,
Looms will sink to sinister rest ;
Tramp in the main street workers' battalions
With red birds soaring high in the air.
Stand we together, who can against us ?
Barring our way, way now so sure ?
Through hands of censor escaping, this angry
Song, like a spark, shoots down towards Lodz.

Vwadiswav Bronievski.

[21]

HUESCA

HEART of the heartless world,
Dear heart, the thought of you
Is the pain at my side,
The shadow that chills my view.

The wind rises in the evening,
Reminds that autumn is near.
I am afraid to lose you,
I am afraid of my fear.

On the last mile to Huesca,
The last fence for our pride,
Think so kindly, dear, that I
Sense you at my side.

And if bad luck should lay my strength
Into the shallow grave,
Remember all the good you can;
Don't forget my love.

John Cornford.

THE DAWN

THE New York dawn has
four columns of mud
and a hurricane of black doves
that dabble in stagnant waters;

The New York dawn moans
upon the tremendous stairways,
seeking amidst the ledges
the nards of clear-etched agony.

The dawn arrives yet none receives it in his mouth.
For in this place there is no morrow, no can be of any hope :
At times come furious swarms of coins
that riddle and devour abandoned children.

The first to rise feel in their bones
that here shall be no paradise nor love stripped of its leaf :
they know their destination, a heaven full of laws and numbers,
the artless games, the fruitless sweat.

With chains and rumours is the light entombed
in the shameless challenge of a rootless science.
In the suburbs are people who sway sleeplessly
like those new-risen from a bloody shipwreck.

Federico Garcia Lorca.
(Translated from the Spanish by A. L. LLOYD.)

ACRES OF POWER

ACRES of power within me lie,
Charted fields of wheat and rye
And behind them, charted too,
Brooding woods of beech and yew.
Beyond them stretch, uncharted yet,
Marsh and mountain, dark and wet,
Whence sometimes in my dream and ease
Strange birds appear among the trees.

The fields of corn are action's fruit,
Gripping the earth with puny root,
Their surface pattern neatly planned
Upon the chaos of my land.
Against the ruminating wood
They set a fence, but to no good ;

[23]

The shadow and the sap of mind
Still weights the harvest of my hand.

And the wild marshes and the hills
Shut out by the imposing will
Yet hurl their livid forms across
To smash the fence and flood the fosse
And all his dictates and his laws
Cannot restrain that surging force,
For the whole land is my power still,
Divided, fenced, but no less real.

And one man only mourning goes
By day through the stiff planted rows,
By night through the tangled wood, to gaze
On the vast savage wilderness.
The born surveyor, he that would
Turn the whole acreage to good,
Subject to one coherent plan
Dispensing the whole power of man.

But he between the fences dour,
This organizer of my power,
By rigid areas is confined
That sever impulse, hand and mind.
For he is only paid to see
That the fields grow obediently
And that the woods do not encroach
Nor the trees part to show the marsh.

For if the power that lavish there
Breaks into a sterile air,
Were planned and planted, fibre and juice,
And all my earth enlaced with use,
Then evil for his ruler's case
Whom to maintain in idleness
My fields of power are bought and sold
And all their goodness changed for gold.

Thus the land that is my life
Divided, ruled, and held in fief,
All the power it could produce
He cannot sell, but I could use.
And my surveyor, grim and harsh,
In secret now reclaims the marsh
That cultivated acres there
May bear a fruit for all to share.

Randall   Swingler.

POEM

AND love hung still as crystal over the bed
    And filled the corners of the enormous room ;
The boom of dawn that left her sleeping, showing
    The flowers mirrored in the mahogany table.

O my love, if only I were able
    To protract this hour of quiet after passion,
Not ration happiness but keep this door for ever
    Closed on the world, its own world closed within it.

But dawn's waves trouble with the bubbling minute
    The names of books come clear upon their shelves,
The reason delves for duty and you will wake
    With a start and go on living on your own.

The first train passes and the windows groan,
    Voices will hector and your voice become
A drum in tune with theirs, which all last night
    Like sap that fingered through a hungry tree
Asserted our one night's identity.

Louis   MacNeice.

SONG

Bells of Cordoba
in the early morning,
And in Granada
bells of the dawn

Moving the maidens
to tears with the gentle
sorrowing tune.
Moving the maidens
of Andalucia
the High and the Low.

All Spanish maidens
with tiny feet,
with skirts that ripple
and trembling sweet,
filling with lights
the crowded street.

O bells of Cordoba
in the early morning,
And o, in Granada,
bells of the dawn!

Federico Garcia Lorca.
(*Translated from the Spanish by* STANLEY RICHARDSON.)

SPEECH FROM A PLAY

Civilisation which was sweet
With love and words, after earthquakes
Terrifies ; architraves
Or flowering leaf of the Corinthian capitol

[26]

Momently threaten ; then fall
In marble waves on life. What was
The fastened mouth of the live past
Speaking in stone against the cloud, becomes
Our present death. O you
Whose thought—pathic through fear and greed—
Has frozen to that brittle shape
Dictated by what's actual in the world,
Which now breaks over us in all-destroying
Crash of injustice, know that your mental images
Are wailings of the falling cities
And photographs of battlefields. But you
Who still will live, dispart
The spiritual will from the material
Ruling pattern of rigid memory
And the system that haunts, to hew what's solid
After the living thought, not think what the dead have willed.
The mountain streams that have electric roots,
The stones
And metals, all of them our plant :
We'll tear from where they stick in minds
Now their possessors ; give them as a prize
To those who've worked in fields and factories
For many centuries.
Into the image of a heart
That feeds separate functions with blood they need
For what they make, we'll shape the wealth
Of the dispossessed world and let those riches pour
Their fertilizing river delta
Across the starved sand of the peoples.
Fall marble, fall decay : but rise
Will of life in brothers : build
Stones in the form of justice : not justice
Into the fall of funeral monuments.

Stephen Spender.

MAN, TAKE YOUR GUN

MAN, take your gun : and put to shame
earthquake and plague, the acts of God.
You maim the crazy and the lame.

Terror is their palsy, the knees
of men buckle for fear of man.
You are the God whom frenzy pleases.

You are the gas-man, and the flier
who drops his bomb ; the man in tanks.
You wire mines and fear the fire.

And dig the hollow street with trenches
the gas-main and the sewer cross.
The stench of dead men makes you flinch.

But if the dying whimper, pain
pricks you like courage, like delight.
The vein sings to the cruel brain.

What are you, man, that gun in hand
with savagery and pity go,
and face to face with madness stand ;

and acid-drenched and poisoned-sprayed
see flame run lovely like a wake
from raiders ; and the burning lake
shake overhead ? You are afraid.

The shadow flickers on the wall
like morse, like gun-shot. Terror walks
the tall roofs where the snipers hawk.
He stalks you, man. And, man, you fall.

J. Bronowski.

THE SPANISH HANDS

THE Spanish hands are young and pitiful.
Captured by disciplined and certain men,
On their own farms
Dejectedly they stand. Manhood
Has not mastered yet their boy's material,
And in their forms
The land's hard-broken awkwardness is shown.

They will be shot. The guns point whiteless eyes
That blacken memories. Each weather of the earth
That had its manual sign
And earth's exactions made futility.
Those simple groups unchanged, the walls and trees
Of their habitual scene
Shall grant no recognition to their death.

The spade thrown down, utensils of the field
Daily familiar with their hands, discarded place ;
And taken, implements
Of other kinds and for another use.
They rose against the nameless will of death,
Moving as winters will across their land,
Themselves to be the devastated yield
And ruined increment :
Knowing that in time's round
There would return for them no further season,
Balanced on arms and boughs, their lives' and summer's unison.

L. J. Yates.

PALAIS DES BEAUX ARTS

ABOUT suffering they were never wrong,
The Old Masters : how well they understood

Its human position; how it takes place
While someone else is eating or opening a window or just walking
              dully along;
How, when the aged are reverently passionately waiting
For the miraculous birth there always must be
Children, who did not specially want it to happen, skating
On a pond at the edge of the wood:
They never forget
That even the dreadful martyrdom must run its course
Anyhow in a corner, some untidy spot
Where the dogs go on with their doggy life, and the torturer's horse
Scratches its innocent behind on a tree.
In Breughel's Icarus, for instance: how everything turns away
Quite leisurely from the disaster; the ploughman may
Have heard the splash, the forsaken cry,
But for him it was not an important failure; the sun shone,
As it had to, on the white legs disappearing into the green
Water; and the expensive delicate ship that must have seen
Had somewhere to get to, and sailed calmly on.

W. H. Auden.

THE NOVELIST

ENCASED in talent like a uniform,
The rank of every poet is well known;
They can amaze us like a thunderstorm,
Or die so young, or live for years alone;

They can dash forward like hussars: but he
Must struggle out of his boyish gift, and learn
How to be plain and backward, how to be
One after whom none think it worth to turn.

For, to achieve his lightest wish, he must
Become the whole of boredom; subject to
Vulgar complaints like love; among the Just

Be just; among the Filthy filthy too;
And in his own weak person, if he can,
Must suffer dully all the wrongs of man.

W. H. Auden.

SNOW IN EUROPE

OUT of their slumber Europeans spun
Dense dreams : appeasement, miracle, glimpsed flash
Of a new golden era ; but could not restrain
The vertical white weight that fell last night
And made their continent a blank.

Hush, says the sameness of the snow.
The Ural and the Jura now rejoin
The furthest Arctic's desolation. All is one
Sheer monotone : plain, mountain : country, town :
Contours and boundaries no longer show.

The warring flags hang colourless a while ;
Now midnight's icy zero feigns a truce
Between the signs and seasons, and fades out
All shots and cries. But when the great thaw comes,
How red shall be the melting snow, how loud the drums!

David Gascoyne.

ELEGY

NEVERTHELESS when the hands cross at midnight and noon
O golden oil spills and from the wheels' mesh
Time produces its patterns of fate on the flesh,

And I shall fall out like golden oil from the clash.
Not then, though, the axle cracks or the wheels veer
           To miss my skull—
I feel the jewelled rims riding up my skin
To leave me drawn and quartered in the rear.

   O may I mourn the mathematics of man
   Who when alone is lovely as the solitary tree
   Evolving existence in an algebra of leaves
   Against the thunderstorm and the appalling flash :
           He is a magnificent one,
But the many of man makes darkness and deceives
Each other with shadow, so that none can see
           The human for the flesh.

   Where shall the unicorn rest
     But in this green breast, where
Mystery is moss and charity is care
           Warm to despair ?
Where else shall sleep the innocent hind
           But in this hand,
Or the lizard and snake lonely from danger
           But along this finger ?

Also Sheffield and South Shields shall rust and rot,
           Northumberland crumble, and Durham moulder,
Without the forge of his forehead to keep them hot
           And his back to shoulder them.
Europe, the jig-saw puzzle, without his great grip
           Collapses through the map,
And mad America, without his grand insanity,
           Be sane as a cemetery.

But blood's on his head and a gun's in his hand :
   It's a suicide that he also threatens
With a shot of war put a stop to his grief
           Whose monument is Europe.
Where the broken column and the laurel garland,

The violin that wails as the sky darkens,
The capital cities lying under gas like a wreath,
Entomb his hope.

Therefore be generous among friends with kisses,
Hold parties of domestic dance and song—
O make the doomed roof ring!
Join me in celebrating the occasions of bliss
That turned a condemned house to a gay room
Ballooned with laughter and ribboned with love.
The lights will go out soon
And the sound of the mooning bomber drone above.

George Barker.

PLACE OF BIRTH

From Winchester the road was dazed with heat ;
after the droughty downs the lanes were night
and drowned in leaves across their caky ruts :
down through the hedge's tunnel and the dust
lay my small village huddling in its trees.

Unmoved since twenty-two its settled houses
however tiny to my later eyes ;
the fields the trees the bushes seemed the same
as when I left them in that dreaded April :
and though the men were dead or gone to Norwich
the women bedridden, the children married,
yet with the known road under my older feet
familiar cowsheds and remembered lanes,
swooped back to me those misty years
when Hampshire was my home and London lovely.

The cottage squatted in its tangled garden
condemned for years to rot and sink ;

the thatch was mossy and the well was rust
the hollow hogweed grew beside the barn
where the late sun was silting through the cracks ;
and redhead docks stood in the living-room
against the curling paper on the wall
towards the ceiling's plaster and its stains :
I picked a plum from the forgotten tree
and wordless smells hung in the evening air,
telling me I was eight, the school was finished,
through the long grass the twisty path, and home
was the small chimney down the valley's blue.

Here I was reared : these fields were mine for running
these beechy lanes my setting and my soil :
a solemn boy with knees and canvas satchels . . .
the milkcan handle cold in Christmas snow,
the plovers howling ghosts against the wind :
the larches in the copse were paintbox colours
and the red admirals hovered in the ivy ;
the autumn brought its gleaning in the stubble
and apples drooping by the window pane.

This was my world, this unconsidered corner,
and a long journey was a league away
though fields to Baybridge or to Fisher's Pond :
London was at the Pole, a kindly giant
with angel porters and tremendous trams :
and here I watched and walked, while vast unknown
history swept by, and blood in Ireland,
war on the Soviets, Sacco in his gaol,
crisis, indemnities, putsches and revolts . . .
and I unseeing in my woods, happy in knowing
peace on the skyline and the future firm.

We weep for what is gone : my dying dog
is the pathetic puppy in the market cage ;
never again that long oblivious calm
and yet our tears for loss, the dying years

the sun and colour of the spacious past :
and tonight's misty trees and mackerel sky
remembered in the draughty days to come
tearing at hearts shaken by midnight guns.

Peter Hewett.

LABOUR EXCHANGE

THESE men, clutching cards, stand in slack groups
Round the stove in the wooden room, fog
Shoving its dim nose around the door.

The clock keeps a prim eye on them, intent
On supervision, and white with disapproval of
Their profane disillusion and their thick mirth.

They have had a slice of bread and lard ;
Warmed their hands at a cup of tea ;
Left wives scrubbing in aprons of sacking,

For this, the terminus of hopes and sorrows,
Where the blazing stadium and the satisfaction of food,
Or the cipher of want, daily arrive and depart.

They stand for many hours, obscure,
Glimpsing through windows the autumn sun on
The spires of the world they built, but do not share.

Clifford Dyment.

LYING TOGETHER

LYING together was sun's warmth to seed
Concealed within our bodies which are worlds

That feed upon our sensualities.
We are the wombs of secret pregnancies
Time slyly rears ; we do not guess
What children we shall bear, what foetus folds
Inside our flesh to make uncertain certainties.
I must have slept like Adam while this love
Grew underneath my ribs in quiet industry.
Our pleasures were too modest for such parentage.
How many simple acts know they connect
Like levers with a vast machinery ?
Yet we have made this child whose cries were forced
One night upon me in its orphan birth.
Pity my pain and save new life from death.

Robert Waller.

REFUGEE BLUES

SAY this city has ten million souls,
Some are living in mansions, some are living in holes ;
Yet there's no place for us, my dear, yet there's no place for us.

Once we had a country and we thought it fair,
Look in the atlas and you'll find it there ;
We can never go there now, my dear, we can never go there now.

The consul banged the table and said :
' If you've no passport, you're officially dead ' ;
But we are still alive, my dear, but we are still alive.

Down in the churchyard there stands an old yew,
Every spring it flowers anew ;
Old passports can't do that, my dear, old passports can't do that.

Went to a committee; they offered me a chair,
Told me politely to come back next year;
But where shall we go today, my dear, but where shall we go
       today?

Came to a public meeting; the speaker got up and said:
'If we let them in, they will steal our daily bread';
He was talking of you and me, my dear, he was talking of you
       and me.

Heard a noise like thunder rumbling in the sky,
It was Hitler over Europe saying, 'They must die!'
O we were in his mind, my dear, O we were in his mind.

Saw a poodle in a jacket, fastened with a pin,
Saw a door open and a cat let in:
But they weren't German Jews, my dear, but they weren't German
       Jews.

Went down to the harbour and stood upon the quay,
Saw the fish swimming as if they were free;
Only ten feet away, my dear, only ten feet away.

Walked into a wood; there were birds in the trees,
They had no politicians and sang at their ease;
They weren't the human race, my dear, they weren't the human
       race.

Dreamt I saw a building with a thousand floors,
A thousand windows and a thousand doors;
Not one of them was ours, my dear, not one of them was ours.

Ran down to the station to catch the express,
Asked for two tickets to Happiness;
But every coach was full, my dear, but every coach was full.

Stood on a great plain in the falling snow,
Ten thousand soldiers marched to and fro,
Looking for you and me, my dear, looking for you and me.

W. H. Auden.

NOW LIKE A LANDSCAPE

Now like a landscape the memory
My wishes inherited
Draws into distance left and right :
And what is past is not dead.

I shall remember him and his words
When the scene changes again ;
The green plateau or the sudden house
Capturing the windowed train

Are just the signals that the traveller
Needs for his reassurance
That death will never distort the scenes
Where his presence still may chance.

Here in this plushed compartment's ease
Two of my best loved ones lie
And count the familiarity
Of field and town running by.

The guarded entry to Micheldever
Where the white clash of chalk face
After the depth of the tunnel's blackness
Startles the eye like a race ;

Or for an instant beyond Winchester
The arterial road alone
Threatens the cathedral as a dart
Cracking into its high stone.

Inviolate as real memory
This lovely, empty landscape
Proves for the searching mind and the eye
His death is not an escape.

Bernard Gutteridge.

FRENCH LISETTE: A BALLAD OF MAIDA VALE

WHO strolls so late, for mugs a bait,
In the mists of Maida Vale,
Sauntering past a stucco gate
Fallen, but hardly frail?

You can safely bet that it's French Lisette,
The Pearl of Portsdown Square,
On the game she has made her name
And rather more than her share.

In a coat of coney with her passport phoney
She left her native haunts,
For an English surname exchanging *her* name
And then took up with a ponce.

Now a meaning look conceals the hook
Some innocent fish will swallow,
Chirping ' Hullo, darling! ' like a cheeky starling
She'll turn, and he will follow,

For her eyes are blue and her eyelids too
And her smile's by no means cryptic,
Her perm's as firm as if waved with glue,
She plies an orange lipstick,

And orange-red is her perky head
Under a hat like a tiny pie—
A pie on a tart, it might be said,
Is redundant, but oh, how spry!

From the distant tundra to snuggle under her
Chin a white fox was conveyed,
And with winks and leerings and Woolworth earrings
She's all set up for trade.

Now who comes here replete with beer?
A quinquagenarian clerk
Who in search of Life has left ' the wife '
And ' the kiddies ' in Tufnell Park.

Dear sir, beware! for sex is a snare
And all is not true that allures.
Good sir, come off it! She means to profit
By this little weakness of yours:

Too late for alarm! Exotic charm
Has caught in his gills like a gaff,
He goes to his fate with a hypnotized gait,
The slave of her silvery laugh,

And follows her in to her suite of sin,
Her self-contained bower of bliss,
They enter her flat, she takes his hat,
And he hastens to take a kiss.

Ah, if only he knew that concealed from view
Behind a ' folk-weave ' curtain
Is her fancy man, called Dublin Dan,
His manner would be less certain,

His bedroom eyes would express surprise,
His attitude less languor,
He would watch his money, not call her ' Honey ',
And be seized with fear or anger.

Of the old technique one need scarcely speak,
But oh, in the quest for Romance
'Tis folly abounding in a strange surrounding
To be divorced from one's pants.

William Plomer.

MEETING POINT

TIME was away and somewhere else,
There were two glasses and two chairs
And two people with the one pulse
(Somebody stopped the moving stairs) :
Time was away and somewhere else,

And they were neither up nor down,
The stream's music did not stop
Flowing through heather, limpid brown,
Although they sat in a coffee shop
And they were neither up nor down.

The bell was silent in the air
Holding its inverted poise—
Between the clang and clang, a flower,
A brazen calyx of no noise :
The bell was silent in the air.

The camels crossed the miles of sand
That stretched around the cups and plates;
The desert was their own, they planned
To portion out the stars and dates :
The camels crossed the miles of sand.

Time was away and somewhere else.
The waiter did not come, the clock
Forgot them, and the radio waltz
Came out like water from a rock :
Time was away and somewhere else.

Her fingers flicked away the ash
That bloomed again in tropic trees :
Not caring if the markets crash
When they had forests such as these,
Her fingers flicked away the ash.

God or whatever means the Good
Be praised, that time can stop like this,
That what the heart has understood
Can verify in the body's peace
God or whatever means the Good.

Time was away and she was here
And life no longer what it was,
The bell was silent in the air
And all the room aglow because
Time was away and she was here.

Louis MacNeice.

ENGLAND
(*Autumn* 1938)

PLUSH bees above a bed of dahlias ;
    Leisurely, timeless garden teas ;
Brown bread and honey ; scent of mowing ;
    The still green light below tall trees.

The ancient custom of deception ;
    A Press that seldom stoops to lies—
Merely suppresses truth and twists it,
    Blandly corrupt and slyly wise.

The Common Man ; his mask of laughter ;
  His back-chat while the roof falls in ;
Minorities' long losing battles
  Fought that the sons of sons may win.

    The politician's inward snigger
      (Big business on the private phone) ;
    The knack of sitting snug on fences ;
      The double face of flesh and stone.

Grape-bloom of distant woods at dusk ;
  Storm-crown on Glaramara's head ;
The fire-rose over London night ;
  An old plough rusting autumn-red.

    The ' incorruptible policeman '
      Gaoling the whore whose bribe's run out,
    Guarding the rich against the poor man,
      Guarding the Settled Gods from doubt.

The generous smile of music-halls
  Bars and bank-holidays and queues ;
The private peace of public foes ;
  The truce of pipe and football news.

    The smile of privilege exultant ;
      Smile at the ' bloody Red ' defeated ;
    Smile at the striker starved and broken ;
      Smile at the ' dirty nigger ' cheated.

The old hereditary craftsman ;
  The incommunicable skill ;
The pride in long-loved tools, refusal
  To do the set job quick or ill.

    The greater artist mocked, misflattered ;
      The lesser forming clique and team
    Or crouching in his narrow corner,
      Narcissus with his secret dream.

England of rebels—Blake and Shelley ;
  England where freedom's sometimes won,
Where Jew and Negro needn't fear yet
  Lynch-law and pogrom, whip and gun.

    England of cant and smug discretion ;
      England of wagecut-sweatshop-knight,
    Of sportsman-churchman-slum-exploiter,
      Of puritan grown sour with spite.

England of clever fool, mad genius,
  Timorous lion and arrogant sheep,
Half-hearted snob and shamefaced bully,
  Of hands that wake and eyes that sleep. . . .
England the snail that's shod with lightning. . . .
  Shall we laugh or shall we weep ?

A. S. J. Tessimond.

THE LEAVES OF LIFE

UNDERNEATH the leaves of life
Green on the prodigious tree,
  In a trance of grief
Stand the fallen man and wife :
Far away the single stag
Banished to a lonely crag
Gazes placid out to sea,
While from thickets round about
Breeding animals look in
  On Duality,
And the birds fly in and out
  Of the world of Man.

Down in order from the ridge,
Bayonets glittering in the sun,
　　Soldiers who will judge
Wind towards the little bridge:
Even politicians speak
Truths of value to the weak,
Necessary acts are done
By the ill and the unjust;
But the Judgment and the Smile,
　　Though these Two-in-One
See creation as they must,
　　None shall reconcile.

Bordering our middle earth
Kingdoms of the Short and Tall,
　　Rivals for our Faith,
Stir up envy from our birth:
So the giant who storms the sky
In an angry wish to die
Wakes the hero in us all,
While the tiny with their power
To divide and hide and flee,
　　When our fortunes fall,
Tempt to a belief in our
　　Immortality.

Lovers running each to each
Feel such timid dreams catch fire
　　Blazing as they touch,
Learn what love alone can teach:
Happy on a tousled bed
Praise Blake's acumen who said:
'One thing only we require
Of each other; we must see
In another's lineaments
　　Gratified desire;
That is our humanity;
　　Nothing else contents.'

Nowhere else could I have known
Than, beloved, in your eyes,
    What we have to learn,
That we love ourselves alone :
All our terrors burned away
We can learn at last to say :
' All our knowledge comes to this,
That existence is enough,
That in savage solitude
    Or the play of love
Every living creature is
    Woman, Man and Child.'

W. H. Auden.

IN MEMORIAM ERNST TOLLER

The shining neutral summer has no voice
To judge America or ask why a man dies ;
And the friends who are sad and the enemies who rejoice

Are chased by their shadows lightly away from the grave
Of one who was egotistical and brave,
Lest they think they can learn without suffering how to forgive.

What was it, Ernst, that your shadow unwittingly said ?
O did the child see something horrid in the woodshed
Long ago ? Or had the Europe which took refuge in your head

Already been too injured to get well ?
O for how long, like the swallows flying in the other cell,
Had the bright little longings been flying in to tell

About the big and friendly death outside
Where people do not travel, occupy or hide ;
No towns like Munich ; no need to write ?

Dear Ernst, lie shadowless at last among
The other war-horses who existed till they'd done
Something that was an example to the young.

We are lived by powers we pretend to understand :
They arrange our loves ; it is they who direct at the end
The sickness, the enemy bullet, or even our hand.

It is their tomorrow hangs over the earth of the living
And all that we wish for our friends : but existence is believing
We know for whom we mourn, and who is grieving.

W. H. Auden.

SONG OF THE AUSTRIANS IN DACHAU

Pitiless the barbed wire dealing
Death that round our prison runs,
And a sky that knows no feeling
Sends us ice and burning suns ;
Lost to us the world of laughter,
Lost our homes, our loves, our all ;
Through the dawn our thousands muster,
To their work in silence fall.

But the slogan of Dachau is burnt on our brains
And unyielding as steel we shall be ;
Are we men, brother ? Then we'll be men when they've done
Work on, we'll go through with the task we've begun,
For work, brother, work makes us free.

Haunted by the gun mouths turning
All our days and nights are spent ;
Toil is ours—the way we're learning
Harder than we ever dreamt ;

Weeks and months we cease to reckon
Pass, and some forget the years,
And so many men are broken
And their faces charged with fears.

But the slogan of Dachau is burnt on our brains, etc.

Heave the stone and drag the truck,
Let no load's oppression show,
In your days of youth and luck
You thought lightly : now you know.
Plunge your spade in earth and shovel
Pity where heart cannot feel,
Purged in your own sweat and trouble
Be yourself like stone and steel.

But the slogan of Dachau is burnt on our brains, etc.

One day sirens will be shrieking
One more roll-call, but the last.
And the stations we'll be seeking—
Outside, brother, prison past!
Bright the eyes of freedom burning,
Worlds to build with joy and zest
And the work begun that morning,
Yes, that work will be our best !

For the slogan of Dachau is burnt on our brains, etc.

(*Note.*—Over the entrance to Dachau Concentration Camp
stood the words : ARBEIT MACHT FREI!)

Georg Anders (*Jura Soyfer.*)
(*Translated by* JOHN LEHMANN.)

[48]

THE WRITER'S HAND

WHAT is your want, perpetual invalid
Whose fist is always beating on my breast's
Bone wall, incurable dictator of my house
And breaker of its peace ? What is your will,
Obscure uneasy sprite : where must I run,
What must I seize, to win
A brief respite from your repining cries ?

Is it a star, the passionate short spark
Produced by friction with another's flesh
You ache more darkly after ? Is it power :
To snap restriction's leash, to leap
Like bloodhounds on the enemy ? There is no grip
Can crush the fate you fight. Or is it to escape
Into the dream perspectives maps and speed create ?

You never listen, disillusion's dumb
To your unheeding ear. But see my hand,
The only army to enforce your claim
Upon life's hostile land : five pale, effete
Aesthetic-looking fingers, whose chief feat
Is to trace lines like these across a page :
What small relief can they bring to your siege!

David Gascoyne.

TIME WILL NOT OPEN HIS CLENCHED HAND

TIME will not open his clenched hand :
there are green shields before the sun ;
over the king and the king's hound
the everlasting sand is sown.

Gods that are falcons, and gods horned,
stir in the mighty loin of rock :
time will not open his clenched hand
—their wings dry, their rods break.
So, in a brooding night of gold,
lie wills unborn, and buried will,
and we—their sole, immortal child
(time will not open his clenched hand)
not dead, but in a life more still ;
spent arrows, in desired land.

Terence Tiller.

THE RESURRECTION OF THE DEAD

MAN's blood, and hope, and human memory
Form the black-tinged ingredients of space
That Daniel's lion-den beneath the smouldering eye
The blue hole of the heavenly throne

The great skies have been raised up like high walls
The black of cracks is outlined by the bluish sheen of steel
The millions of the judgment called, like planets all too pale
With memories of underneath the earth, go flying past

And the harlot seated high upon the waters, and
Downfallen, the great death poured from the cups
And I have seen what blows the heavenly host endures
And the white giant who has a dagger in his mouth

I've seen the only liberty there is vanquished by death
Beneath the swaddling-linen of the sky
Bathed in the black blood of the cups and wounds
When the great harlot of the waters had burst into flame

I was a man ; O now illumine my remains!
And grant me pardon if I lived but for a Beast
And if I was voluptuously in love with lovely Death,
I was the poet : O illumine the whole

And if thou wast not God I will establish still
On Nothing over Nothingness the soul's supremacy,
For God not of the dead but of the living is the God
And no more can they die, the risen dead.

Pierre Jean Jouve.
(*Translated from the French by* DAVID GASCOYNE.)

INSULA MONTI MAJORIS

How tender were the rocks upon the marsh
How hard the rocks were in the rock

How the birds climbed in the eternal sky
How the winds swung to and fro
The summer earth's black essences

How violently those suns beat down upon the plague
How frightened were those hearts
To be deprived of woman's sex
How deeply slept the shadows in the shadow of the stones

How holy was the terror of the day
Around the sounding stone
Their stony modulation was without a fault
They sang

How sepulchral and giant was their soul
That God had pierced with a wound greater than the soul!
How far had they gone out from the woman's womb
And how the odour became sweet out of their tombs!

How black were those white men against the fine day's light
Sleeping yet never asleep
For the Master was in agony always
Until the end of time beneath the glowing sky.

Pierre Jean Jouve.
(Translated from the French by DAVID GASCOYNE.)

WORDS MIGHT BREED TIGERS

WORDS might breed tigers
In the blood
Or light a sun
In the eye :

Thoughts might fire lions
In the loins
Or steel-sinewed panthers
In the mind :

Wrongs might father serpents
On the tongue
Or foundry-blast an eagle
In the brain :

But words, thoughts and wrongs
Have given birth to mules
Or, perhaps, a ligon :
Mules are obstinate, but cheap and strong,
We put the ligon in a cage for fools to spit upon.

Arthur Harvey.

POEM

CRUEL, uncomfortable and blind
Fingers stretch like webs over the mind,
Cover the seeing eyes and the whispering tongue,
Stop the slow and sea-like song
And push up pebbles from the shore.

Now we have met this silent war
With voice and head alike
Bowed to the rage of storm and tear,
And like rain arrows on the lake
The blinding fingers strike and break

Across the comforts of the mind.
O cruel, comfortless and blind,
The dead are walking by like ghosts
And we can only through the mists
See the future striking our uncertain coasts.

Nicholas Moore.

THE WIDOW'S PLOT
Or, She Got What Was Coming to Her

TROUBLED was a house in Ealing
Where a widow's only son
Found her fond maternal feeling
Overdone.

She was fussy and possessive;
Lennie, in his teens,
Found the atmosphere oppressive;
There were scenes.

Tiring one day of her strictures
Len went down the street,
Took a ticket at the pictures,
            Took his seat.

The picture was designed to thrill,
But oh, the girl he sat beside!
If proximity could kill
            He'd have died.

Simple, sweet, sixteen and blonde,
Unattached, her name was Bess.
Well, boys, how would *you* respond?
            I can guess.

Len and Bessie found each other
All that either could desire,
But the fat, when he told Mother,
            Was in the fire.

The widow who had always dreaded
This might happen, hatched a scheme
To bust, when they were duly wedded,
            Love's young dream.

One fine day she murmured, ' Sonny,
It's not for me to interfere,
You may think it rather funny
            But I hear

Bess goes out with other men.'
' I don't believe it! It's a lie!
Tell me who with, where, and when!
            Tell me why! '

' Keep cool, Lennie. I suspected
That the girl was far from nice.
What a pity you rejected
            My advice.'

Suspicion from this fatal seed
Sprang up overnight
And strangled, like a poisonous weed,
      The lilies of delight.

Still unbelieving, Len believed
That Bess was being unchaste,
And a man that feels himself deceived
      May act in haste.

Now Bess was innocence incarnate
And never thought of other men;
She visited an aunt at Barnet
      Now and then,

But mostly stayed at home and dusted,
Crooning early, crooning late,
Unaware of being distrusted
      By her mate.

Then one day a wire was sent:
MEET ME PALACEUM AT EIGHT
URGENT AUNTIE. Bessie went
      To keep the date.

Slightly anxious, Bessie came
To the unusual rendezvous.
Desperate, Lennie did the same,
      He waited too,

Seeing but unseen by Bessie,
And in a minute seeing red—
For a stranger, fat and dressy,
      A trilby on his head,

In his tie a tasteful pearl,
On his face a nasty leer,
Sidled up towards the girl
      And called her ' Dear.'

At this juncture Len stepped in,
Made a bee-line for the lout,
With a straight left to the chin
    Knocked him out.

He might have done the same for Bess
Thinking still that she had tricked him,
But she was gazing in distress
    At the victim.

' It's a *her !* ' she cried (but grammar
Never was her strongest suit) :
' She's passed out ! ' he heard her stammer :
    ' Lennie, scoot! '

' It's *what ?* A *her ?* Good God, it's *Mum !*
Ah, now I see! A wicked plan
To make me think my Bess had come
    To meet a man——'

' Now what's all this ? ' a copper said,
Shoving the crowd aside. ' I heard a
Rumour somebody was dead.
    Is it murder ? '

Len quite candidly replied,
' No, officer, it's something less.
It's justifiable matricide,
    Isn't it, Bess ? '

William Plomer.

THE POET

For me there is no dismay
Though ills enough impend.
I have learned to count each day

Minute by breathing minute—
Birds that lightly begin it,
Shadows muting its end—
As lovers count for luck
Their own heart-beats and believe
In the forest of time they pluck
Eternity's single leaf.

Tonight the moon's at the full.
Full moon's the time for murder.
But I look to the clouds that hide her—
The bay below me is dull,
An unreflecting glass—
And chafe for the clouds to pass,
And wish she suddenly might
Blaze down at me so I shiver
Into a twelve-branched river
Of visionary light.

For now imagination,
My royal, impulsive swan,
With raking flight—I can see her—
Comes down as it were upon
A lake in whirled snow-floss
And flurry of spray like a skier
Checking. Again I feel
The wounded waters heal.
Never before did she cross
My heart with such exaltation.

Oh, on this striding edge,
This hare-bell height of calm
Where intuitions swarm
Like nesting gulls and knowledge
Is free as the winds that blow,
A little while sustain me,
Love, till my answer is heard!
Oblivion roars below,

Death's cordon narrows : but vainly,
If I've slipped the carrier word.

Dying, any man may
Feel wisdom harmonious, fateful
At the tip of his dry tongue.
All I have felt or sung
Seems now but the moon's fitful
Sleep on a clouded bay,
Swan's maiden flight, or the climb
To a tremulous, hare-bell crest.
Love, tear the song from my breast!
Short, short is the time.

C. Day Lewis.

THE SILENT LAND

THE mountains are empty. No hermits have hallowed the caves,
Nor has the unicorn drunk from the green fountain
Whose poplar shadow never heard the horn.
Lives like a vanishing nightdew drop away.

The sea casts up its wreckage, ship or shell,
Beams of day and darkness guardedly
Break on the savage forests that from groins
And armpits of the hills so fiercely look.

The plains are nameless and the cities cry for meaning,
The unproved heart still seeks a vein of speech
Beside the sprawling rivers, in the stunted township,
By the pine windbreak where the hot wind bleeds.

Man must lie with the gaunt hills like a lover,
Earning their intimacy in the calm sigh

Of a century of quiet and assiduity,
Discovering what solitude has meant

Before our headlong time broke on these waters,
And in himself unite time's dual order;
For he to both the swift and slow belongs,
Formed for a hard and complex history.

So relenting, earth will tame her tamer,
And speak with all her voices tenderly
To seal his homecoming to the world. Ah then
For him the Oreads will haunt the fields near the snow-line,

He will walk with his shadow across the bleaching plain
No longer solitary, and hear the sea talking
Dark in the rocks, O and the angel will visit,
Signing life's air with indefinable mark.

Charles Brasch.
(New Zealand.)

LARCH TREE

Oh, larch tree with scarlet berries
sharpen the morning slender sun
sharpen the thin taste of September
with your aroma of sweet wax and powder delicate.

Fruit is falling in the valley
breaking on the snouts of foxes
breaking on the wooden crosses
where children bury the shattered bird.

Fruit is falling in the city
blowing a woman's eyes and fingers
across the street among the bones
of boys who could not speak their love.

[59]

I watch a starling cut the sky
a dagger through the blood of cold
and grasses bound by strings of wind
stockade the sobbing fruit among the bees.

Oh, larch tree, with icy hair
your needles thread the thoughts of snow
while in the fields a shivering girl
takes to her breasts the sad ripe apples.

Laurie Lee.

JUNIPER

Juniper holds to the moon
a girl adoring a bracelet;
as the hills draw up their knees
they throw off their jasmine girdles.

You are a forest of game,
a thought of nights in procession,
you tread through the bitter fires
of the nasturtium.

I decorate you to a smell of apples,
I divide you among the voices
of owls and cavaliering cocks
and woodpigeons monotonously dry.

I hang lanterns on your mouth
and candles from your passionate crucifix,
and bloody leaves of the virginia
drip with their scarlet oil.

There is a pike in the lake
whose blue teeth eat the midnight stars
piercing the water's velvet skin
and puncturing your sleep.

I am the pike in your breast,
my eyes of clay revolve the waves
while cirrus roots and lilies grow
between our banks of steep embraces.

Laurie Lee.

OPEN THE DOOR

DEATH is frozen waiting at my door.
Open to him! Open the door!
Because I still have a soul in my breast!
This morning, as I was passing by, the cypresses
Presented arms
And the wet earth longed for
The handful of my dust.
Let us open and receive Death!
Because I still have a soul in my breast.
The standing furrows that I ploughed
This year also expect my sowing.

Pantelis Prevelakis.
(*Translated from the Greek by* D. CAPETANAKIS.)

NO ORPHEUS, NO EURYDICE

NIPPLES of bullets, precipices,
Ropes, knives, all
Now would seem as gentle

[61]

As the far away kisses
Of her these days remove
—To the mad dervish of his mind
Lost to her love.

There where his thoughts alone
At night dance round his walls,
They paint his pale darling
In a piteous attitude standing
Amongst winds of cold space,
Dead, and waiting in sweet grace
For him to follow when she calls.

For how can he believe
Her loss less than his?
' True it is that she did leave
Me for another's kiss;
Yet our lives did so entwine
That the blank space of my heart
Torn from hers apart,
Tore hers too from mine.'

O, but if he started
Upon that long journey
Of the newly departed
Where one and all are born poor
Into death naked,
Like a slum Bank Holiday
Of bathers on a desolate shore;

If, with nerves strung like a harp
He searched amongst the spirits there
Looking and singing for his wife
To follow him back into life
Out of this dull leaden place,
He would never find there
Her cold, starry, wondering face.

For he is no Orpheus,
She no Eurydice.
She has truly packed and gone
To live with someone
Else, in the pleasures of the sun,
Far from his kingdoms of despair
Here, there or anywhere.

Stephen Spender.

IN MEMORIAM

THE senseless drone of the dull machines in the sky
    In a chain extending the boundaries
        Of a distant invisible will,
Weaves a net of sound in the blackness on high
Drawing the senses up in one Eye
    From our tunnelled entombed bodies,
Here where everything stops but the wishes that kill.

Living now becomes withered like flowers
    In the boring burned city which has no use
        For us but as lives and deaths to fill
With fury the mouths blazing back on the powers
That scorch our small plot of blasted hours :
    We cannot refuse
Here where everything stops but the wishes that kill.

Driven by intolerance and volted with lies
    We melt down the birdlike bodies of boys
        And their laughter distil
To plough metal hatred through the skies
And write with their burning dreams over cities
    Sure no summer joys,
There where everything stops but the wishes that kill.

Filled with swearing, laughter and fire,
Soothed by a girl's hands and wrapped in my word,
What, my fine feather-head, larking friend Bill,
Was your life but a curving arc of desire
Ricochetting in flames on your own funeral pyre
Instinctive as bird,
Here where everything stops but the wishes that kill ?

Stephen Spender.

THE UNHISTORIC STORY

WHALING for continents suspected deep in the south
The Dutchmen envied the unknown, drew bold
Images of market-place, populous river-mouth,
The Land of Beach ignorant of the value of gold :
Morning in Murderers' Bay,
Blood drifted away.
It was something different, something
Nobody counted on.

Clinging like a fly to cape and clouded snow
Cook prisoned them in islands, turning from planets
His measuring mission, showed what the musket could do,
Made his Christmas goose of the wild gannets.
Still as the collier steered
No continent appeared ;
It was something different, something
Nobody counted on.

The roving tentacles rested, touched, clutched
Substantial earth, that is, accustomed haven
For the hungry whaler. Some inland, some hutched
Rudely in bays, the shaggy foreshore shaven,

Lusted, preached as they knew
But as the children grew
It was something different, something
Nobody counted on.

Green slashed with flags, pipeclay and boots in the bush,
Christ in canoes and the musketed Maori boast;
All a rubble-rattle at Time's glacial push:
Vogel and Seddon howling empire from an empty coast
A vast ocean laughter
Echoed unheard, and after
All it was different, something
Nobody counted on.

The pilgrim dream pricked by a cold dawn died
Among the chemical farmers, the fresh towns; among
Miners, not husbandmen, who piercing the side
Let the land's life, found like all who had so long
Bloodily or tenderly striven
To rearrange the given,
It was something different, something
Nobody counted on.

After all re-ordering of old elements
Time trips up all but the humblest of heart
Stumbling after the fire, not in the smoke of events;
For many are called, but many are left at the start,
And whatever islands may be
Under or over the sea,
It is something different, something
Nobody counted on.

                                        Allen Curnow.
                                        (New Zealand.)

PEN FRIENDS

WHY flaunt your naked heart
In the public printed word?
The pimp who works by post
Is much to be preferred.
Lonely widow, refined,
Musical, blonde, petite,
Homely, but cheery withal,
Genuine, wishes to meet—
You know the sort of thing:
But it's better to come to me
With my motto ' In Confidence '
And my very moderate fee.

Somehow a man must live,
Somehow a man must eat:
I dwell in a modest flat
In an unobtrusive street
And call myself (why not?)
The League of Loyal Mates—
A name that much appeals
To unsophisticates.
They answer my Small Ads
In which I guarantee
To further their desires
For a very moderate fee.

You'd learn a lot about life
If you could see my books
Which list the hankerings
Of sundry cranks and crooks,
The blackmailer's designs,
The aims of parasites,
And appetites grown sharp
For want of love's delights.
But oh, the innocents!

Both old and young suppose
That I can cull for them
Perfection, like a rose.

As the League of Loyal Mates
I put each one in touch
With another who may suit—
If not, does it matter much ?
The simple soldier seeks
The girl-wife of a dream ;
The speculator wants
A partner in a scheme
(A partner, be it said,
Equipped with ready cash) ;
The spinster longs at last
To try and cut a dash ;

The lecher hopes to find
The pander to his lust,
And the woman thrice deceived
A man at last to trust :
Well, sometimes they succeed,
They write to me and say,
' Dear Sir, All thanks to you
Lady Luck has come to stay . . .'
' No guinea, dear League of Mates,
Was ever better spent . . .'
' With the Vicar's compliments
From the happiest man in Kent . . .'

I *have* known odd results,
For wonders never cease
The League has sometimes been
A help to the police :
They found a miser once
Bisected with an axe
By a Mate whom I'd procured,
So I put them on her tracks.

Somehow a man must live,
And proudly I can boast
The true philanthropy
Of a pimp who works by post.

William Plomer.

THE GRAVEL-PIT FIELD

BESIDE the stolid opaque flow
Of rain-gorged Thames ; beneath a thin
Layer of early-evening light
Which seems to drift, a ragged veil,
Upon the chilly March air's tide :
Upwards in shallow shapeless tiers
A stretch of scurfy pock-marked waste
Sprawls laggardly its acres till
They touch a raw brick-villa'd rim.

Amidst this nondescript terrain
Haphazardly the gravel-pits'
Rough-hewn rust-coloured hollows yawn,
Their steep declivities away
From the field-surface dropping down
Towards the depths below where rain-
Water in turbid pools stagnates
Like scraps of sky decaying in
The sockets of a dead man's stare.

The shabby coat of coarse grass spread
Unevenly across the ruts
And humps of lumpy soil ; the bits
Of stick and threads of straw ; loose clumps
Of weeds with withered stalks and black
Tatters of leaf and scorched pods : all

These intertwined minutiae
Of Nature's humblest growths persist
In their endurance here like rock.

As with untold intensity
On the far edge of Being, where
Life's last faint forms begin to lose
Name and identity and fade
Away into the void, endures
The final thin triumphant flame
Of all that's most despoiled and bare :
So these last stones, in the extreme
Of their abasement might appear

Like rare stones such as could have formed
A necklet worn by the dead queen
Of a great Pharaoh, in her tomb . . .
So each abandoned snail-shell strewn
Among these blotched dock-leaves might seem
In the pure ray shed by the loss
Of all man-measured value, like
Some priceless pearl-enamelled toy
Cushioned on green silk under glass.

And who in solitude like this
Can say the unclean mongrel's bones
Which stick out, splintered, through the loose
Side of a gravel-pit, are not
The precious relics of some saint,
Perhaps miraculous ? Or that
The lettering on this Woodbine-
Packet's remains ought not to read :
Mene mene tekel upharsin ?

Now a breeze gently breathes across
The wilderness's cryptic face ;
The meagre grasses scarcely stir ;
But when some stronger gust sweeps past,

[69]

Seeming as though an unseen swarm
Of sea-birds had disturbed the air
With their strong wings' wide stroke, a gleam
Of freshness hovers everywhere
About the field ; and tall weeds shake,

Leaves wave their tiny flags, to show
That the wind blown about the brow
Of this poor plot is nothing less
Than the great constant draught the speed
Of Earth's gyrations makes in Space . . .
As I stand musing, overhead
The Zenith's stark light thrusts a ray
Down through dusk's rolling vapours, casts
A last lucidity of day

Across the scene : And in a flash
Of insight I behold the field's
Apotheosis : No-man's-land
Between this world and the beyond,
Remote from men and yet more real
Than any human dwelling-place :
A tabernacle where one stands
As though within the empty space
Round which revolves the Sages' Wheel.

David Gascoyne.
Spring 1941.

THE FAULT

AFTER the light decision
Made by the blood in a moon-blanched lane,
Whatever weariness or contrition
May come, I could never see you plain ;
No, never again

See you whose body I'm wed to
Distinct, but always dappled, enhanced
By a montage of all that moment led to—
Dunes where heat-haze and sea-pinks glanced,
The roads that danced

Ahead of our aimless car,
Scandal biting the dust behind us,
The feel of being on a luckier star,
Each quarrel that came like a night to blind us
And closer to bind us.

Others will journey over
Our hill up along this lane like a rift
Loaded with moon-gold, many a lover
Sleepwalking through the moon's white drift,
Loved or bereft.

But for me it is love's volcanic
Too fertile fault, and will mark always
The first shock of that yielding mood, where satanic
Bryony twines and frail flowers blaze
Through our tangled days.

                                                C. Day Lewis.

SONG

THE fabulous convinces still, and all the cocks are crowing,
The stars are perched on chimney tops, loudly, loudly chorussing :

' *O the poor are poor because the rich are rich,*
This simple fact we've long been telling ;
So who makes the wars and who dies in the ditch,
It's up to you, for we and the sun and the moon go spinning.'

The stars are perched on aqueducts, and underneath the water
        wander,
They look up at their breaking light, and this chorussing they
        render :

  ' O the rich get richer and the poor get poorer,
  All in the name of religion and the nation ;
  And you can't be so low but you can go lower—
  But don't ask us, find for yourself the sharp correction.'

The stars are circling at the eaves, the southwest wind is blowing,
The fabulous convinces still, and all the cocks are crowing.

Ewart Milne.

VILLAGE OF WINTER CAROLS

VILLAGE of winter carols
and gawdy spinning tops,
of green-handed walnuts
and games in the moon.

You were adventure's web,
the flag of fear I flew
riding black stallions
through the rocky streets.

You were the first faint map
of the mysterious sun,
chart of my island flesh
and the mushroom-tasting kiss.

But no longer do I join
your children's sharp banditti,
nor seek the glamour of
your ravished apples.

Your hillocks build no more
their whales and pyramids,
nor howl across the night
their springing wolves.

For crouching in my brain
the crafty thigh of love
twists your old landscape
with a new device.

And every field has grown
a strange and flowering pit
where I must try the blind
and final trick of youth.

Laurie Lee.

NIGHT OF ACACIAS

Two or three days of love has life : then this withered tree hangs
full of a thousand bees and blossoms,
Like the one night in June when the acacias bloom and die.
The river is wearing a chaplet of lights and is fragrant with em-
balmed bathers,
The streets are suddenly wide and sparkling like beauty shops.
From beyond the river over hanging bridges, with a rosary of lights,
Invisible gardens are on the march, colliding with walkers ;
They're off to their rendezvous with the parks and the alleys of the
central squares and main streets.
Benumbed I do not recognise the old streets of the New City
Whose plain and graceless walls are today majestic as palace courts.

O night of acacias, of fountains and of that treacherous pianissimo,
stay,
Make me for ever yearn for love and for Prague ;
O night at the end of June, short-lived as passionate love, as sensual
delight.

[73]

O night of acacias, do not pass before I have crossed all the bridges
        of Prague
In my search for no one, not a friend, not a woman, not even
        myself.

O night with summer in your wake, I long to breathe unendingly
        your ebon hair;
Your diamonds have bewitched me, I want to look for them in the
        waters, poor fisherman that I am.

Oh if at least I could say au revoir to you,
O night in June,
If I were never to see you again,
Let me dissolve in your embrace, my evil fate, my love.

Vitězslav Nezval.
(*Translated from the Czech by* EWALD OSERS.)

THE MIDDLE OF A WAR

My photograph already looks historic.
The promising youthful face, the matelot's collar,
Say 'This one is remembered for a lyric.
His place and period—nothing could be duller.'

Its position is already indicated—
The son or brother in the album; pained
The expression and the garments dated,
His fate so obviously preordained.

The original turns away; as horrible thoughts,
Loud fluttering aircraft slope above his head
At dusk. The ridiculous empires break like biscuits.

Ah, life has been abandoned by the boats—
Only the trodden island and the dead
Remain, and the once inestimable caskets.

Roy Fuller.

SHOP WINDOW

In the confused magnificence of love
is no community, but unsharing crowds
of shuttered faces where no secrets move ;
but a perpetual early-closing day.
The tender lust that sanctifies our bloods,
that flowered by companionship, the way
of the moth's mind, they neither feel nor speak,
haunted with flames : our world's a spirit-walk.

Behind the dreaming shutters of our faces
the spider fingers thoughts, and we dissect
with sharp artistic hands our gains and losses ;
build the mosaic of a filtered world.
We hang a blinding arras upon the fact,
for wild wild unpardonably wild
the roaring of the outer enmity.
Yet we, being islanded, will draw down that sea.

Never believe us ; poets tell you lies :
the burglar breaks the window, and the door
blows inwards, and the pictures tatter loose.
The snarler with hooked fingers, or the man
with nooses, throw a shadow on the floor.
Sooner or later we shall weep again.
There is no refuge from the teeming road
and the four walkers waiting to be God.

World was not built for dreams, my dear; the dreamer
cores his unsympathy to a navel of gold;
rides home at evening swathed about with clamour,
he in his inward starlight never seeing
commercial colours, or the nervous mould
that hangs their lightning round him. And so being
rapt from humanity, wakes not till their feet
press down his bones to raise up Regent Street.

So our delight will never be alone,
or straight and safe as the lark's tower of air;
familiar things will break it, strange look on
with the fierce laugh of lynchers; and the sea
speak our end in mountains to the shore.
Oh if that future tears us, it will be
but bridal violence. For he loves you still
who leans and weeps upon the window-sill.

Terence Tiller.
Cairo.

MA WICKS

OLD Jock and I
Turn past the way to the barracks, round a sty,
Through taut and skinny bushes
And a dip in the moor like an empty eye,
And worm a way
Through canes, and granny-handed blackberry hedges
That cackle at the late hour of day,
To old Ma Wicks, who nests in a wet hollow
Fizzing with midges.

There
We see whippet mist chase tails in the air
And wrap round the mauve and brittle flags

[76]

That hem her twisted path.
(The door is bent with rain and sun, see—
How it drags.)
Inside, four mangy bitches on her hearth
Grow furs and vigour,
And fatten fast :
All beasts that go decrepit in the wind's rigour,
Turn to her chimney as the sea's one mast.

The khaki that we wear
Is thrown off, and lost behind a chair,
Then Jock and I
Half-doze in tweeds
Once drowned in nearby, murderous pools,
And hear the nibbling muskrats cry,
And watch Ma Wicks, by dark and sonorous stairs,
Tease us with murmuring and scattered words
That sometimes catch the bitches unawares
And start them up, like whitefaced, bullied fools :
And, one by one, we please her with our wiles,
    For each of us is greedy for her care.

Lawrence Little.

EMBARKATION

Squirrel,
Grey tuft of fluff,
You bounce about oblivious of our khaki stuff,
Till sergeant or some striper
Marches too near your tree,
Then, like a discovered sniper
You screech up its mossy shanks
And pant your furry heart through leaves at him
In a petulant huff.

[77]

Squirrel,
You have your brothers :
I saw one's heart get lost in furry shivers.
These boys had soldiering on paper,
Only a spit and polish blimpery ;
Now a corroding death for them, too serious a caper,
Soughs over the rasping sea,
And no leafy and close-at-hand tree
Waits and delivers.

Lawrence Little.

GOODBYE FOR A LONG TIME

A FURNISHED room beyond the stinging of
The sea, reached by a gravel road in which
Puddles of rain stare up with clouded eyes :

The photographs of other lives than ours ;
The scattered evidence of your so brief
Possession ; daffodils fading in a vase.

Our kisses here as they have always been,
Half sensual, half sacred, bringing like
A scent our years together, crowds of ghosts.

And then among the thousand thoughts of parting
The kisses grow perfunctory ; the years
Are waved away by your retreating arm.

And now I am alone. I am once more
The far-off boy without a memory,
Wandering with an empty deadened self.

Suddenly under my feet there is the small
Body of a bird, startling against the gravel.
I see its tight shut eye, a trace of moisture.

And ruffling its gentle breast the wind, its beak
Sharpened by death : and I am yours again,
Hurt beyond hurting, never to forget.

Roy Fuller.

SPRING 1942

ONCE as we were sitting by
The falling sun, the thickening air,
The chaplain came against the sky
And quietly took a vacant chair.

And under the tobacco smoke :
' Freedom,' he said, and ' Good,' and ' Duty.'
We stared as though a savage spoke.
The scene took on a singular beauty.

And we made no reply to that
Obscure, remote communication,
But only stared at where the flat
Meadow dissolved in vegetation.

And thought : O sick, insatiable
And constant lust ; O death, our future ;
O revolution in the whole
Of human use of man and nature!

Roy Fuller.

CONVOY

THE wind is quiet now, low pregnant clouds
Darken the plains of the sea ; but no one sleeps.
The plaintive sirens of the dim-seen convoy
Open the gates of pity like a cry
Of frightened animals when horror glares
Green-eyed, from the black forest all around.

To each of us, closed up at action stations,
The wailful sirens call a special tune—
Sheep in the rocky slopes of clouded fells
In Cumberland, cows in the sun-drenched meads
Of Oxfordshire on summer afternoons—
Loved earth replanted in sea-wearied hearts.
Then a torpedo shatters the still night.
For some of us there is no homecoming.

There is no righteous anger ; only hatred.
Pity those sweating in their fumy cell,
Exiles from stars and winds of evening,
Dreaming, like us, of home ; all warped and gnarled
By their world's rottenness—to call them guilty
Is jangling broken words to no sane end.

Think, till morality gives way to tears,
Of women weeping the long lonely night
In sleepy German towns the tourist loved,
Prisoners pacing each her cell of fear
Within the skull, her daily agony
The postman's knock each morning.

Only by pity, the obstinate heart
That dares be human, may we hope to clean
Some blood from our red fingers ; murderers all,
All whom their heart's consent binds to the war
Share in the killing : spinster patriots,

The parsons urging heaven to mobilize,
And pacifists with all their reservations
Harvesting fields that blood has fertilized.

And now the sea peels silently astern
Into the tattered dawn and now to leave
Enigmas labyrinthine unresolved,
Time's children, all our seeking only yields
Contemporary truth—eyes in the dark ;
Chasing the ultimate Grail of good and ill
All vanity and labour lost. We keep
The truest course by the best light we know.

Norman Hampson.

SONG

THE sea forgets her masters : the seaman
turns from her flashing hair, her green eyes,
strips to the muscle for a harbour leman ;
and smiles when he dies.

The land forgets the reaper : his sickle
burrows in strange corn, his tavern tale
is lewd with names of women who were fickle ;
he laughs, he drinks his ale.

The air forgets her lightning : the thunder
dies in remoter valleys ; the great spout
of spangling water, corn and sea pull under ;
she burns, and there is drought.

Terence Tiller.

VAN GOGH

SEE how the yellow tide rolls the corn,
Blue winds bring the storm,
The whirling suns above the uneasy plain
Strike verticle the centres of pain,
Where the harvest and the trees and the hills
Writhe and swirl in terrible curves.
No longer the drawbridge at Arles,
Or the kind landscapes of Auvers ;
For this the sunflowers rehearse,
Still life before the outline blurs,
Gathers itself closer into burning bands
Of colour under the child's clenched hands
Searing the eyeballs. Louder the bright
Beacon of death, the ravens' flight
The dancing spots upon the brain,
That can no more endure this midsummer of pain.

Robin Atthill.

KILCARTY TO DUBLIN

THE paraffin lamps and the home-cured bacon,
The whitewash misty behind the trees
Are taken apart and sorted and shaken
By a war that rages beyond two seas.
The sweets in the dim shop-window glitter,
The idiot girl still sits in the 'bus :
The literal meaning of all grows bitter
If not for her, then at least for us.
But life goes on in the last lit city
Just in the way it has always done
And pity is lost on the tongues of the witty
And the wolf at the door is a figure of fun.

Maurice James Craig.

A LOVE POEM

Put out the candle, close the biting rose,
For cock and cony are asleep ; the sheep
In her secretive hills, with fleece at peace,
Now lies enfolded.

The hungry sceptre-kissing mouth, the moth
Behind the fingers, no more eat the night ;
The rooting worm has crawled away from play
In his wet burrows.

Now the extremest joys are dreams and toys ;
It's darkness in a vast full-tide abed ;
Over abandoned bodies time shall climb
Like the black spider.

Give memory all amazing hours, all showers
Or sharply pouring seas between the knees ;
Slack as a rope, the flesh is dull, and full
Of its perfection.

And all that lately flashed and leapt is gripped
Into a knot of symbols ; all's grown small,
Quiet as curtains : brave be this your grave,
And fresh your garlands.

Terence Tiller.

WORD OVER ALL

Now when drowning imagination clutches
At old loves drifting away,
Splintered highlights, hope capsized—a wrecked world's
Flotsam, what can I say

To cheer the abysmal gulfs, the crests that lift not
To any land in sight?
How shall the sea-waif, who lives from surge to surge, chart
Current and reef aright?

Always our time's ghost-guise of impermanence
Daunts me : whoever I meet,
Wherever I stand, a shade of parting lengthens
And laps around my feet.
But now, the heart sunderings, the real migrations—
Millions fated to flock
Down weeping roads to mere oblivion—strike me
Dumb as a rooted rock.

I watch when searchlights set the low cloud smoking
Like acid on metal : I start
At sirens, sweat to feel a whole town wince
And thump, a terrified heart,
Under the bomb-strokes. These, to look back on, are
A few hours' unrepose :
But the roofless old, the child beneath the débris—
How can I speak for those?

Busy the preachers, the politicians weaving
Voluble charms around
This ordeal, conjuring a harvest that shall spring from
Our heart's all-harrowed ground.
I, who chose to be caged with the devouring
Present, must hold its eye
Where blaze ten thousand farms and fields unharvested,
And hearts, steel-broken, die.

Yet words there must be, wept on the cratered present,
To gleam beyond it :
Never was cup so mortal but poets with mild
Everlastings have crowned it.
See wavelets and wind-blown shadows of leaves on a stream

How they ripple together,
As life and death intermarried—you cannot tell
One from another.

Our words like poppies love the maturing field,
But form no harvest :
May lighten the innocent's pang, or paint the dreams
Where guilt is unharnessed.
Dark over all, absolving all is hung
Death's vaulted patience :
Words are to set man's joy and suffering there
In constellations.

We speak of what we know, but what we have spoken
Truly we know not—
Whether our good may tarnish, our grief to far
Centuries glow not.
The Cause shales off, the Humankind stands forth
A mightier presence,
Flooded by dawn's pale courage, rapt in eve's
Rich acquiescence.

C. Day Lewis.

CHRYSOTHEMIS

I CANNOT follow them into their world of death,
Or their hunted world of life, though through the house,
Death and the hunted bird sing at every nightfall.
I am Chrysothemis : I sailed with dipping sails,
Suffered the winds I would not strive against,
Entered the whirlpools and was flung outside them,
Survived the murders, triumphs and revenges,
Survived ; and remain in a falling, decaying mansion,
A house detested and dark in the setting sun,
The furniture covered with sheets, the gardens empty,

A brother and a sister long departed,
A railing mother gone.
It is my house now. I have set myself to protect,
Against the demons that linger inside our walls,
Their saddened, quiet children of darkness and shame :
They lie on inherited beds in their heavy slumbers,
Their faces relaxed to nocturnal innocence.
I will protect them in the decaying palace.

In the dying sun, through slots in the shuttered windows,
I can see the hanging gardens carved on our mountain
Above and below us, terraces, groves and arbours,
The careful rise of the trees to meet the heavens,
The deliberate riot of the wilderness,
The silent arch through which my brother returned,
And again returned.

In the long broad days of summer,
On the great hill the house lay, lost and absorbed and dreaming,
The gardens glittered under the sweeping sun,
The inmates kept to their rooms, and hope
Rose in the silence.
                                    And indeed
It seemed the agony must die. But then
The house would seem to sigh, and then again,
A sigh and another silence. Through the slotted shutters
I would see them there, my mother and my sister
Wandering and meeting in the garden's quiet
(And I moved from room to room to see them better).
There seemed a truce between them, as if they had
Called off their troops in order to bury their dead.
I could not hear my sister speak ; but clearly,
She spoke with calm and patience, and my mother gave
The answer designed to please, wistful and eager ;
And her words would be quietly taken, twisted and turned,
Ropes, that would loose the rivers to flood again ;
The fragile dams would burst, indeed constructed
Only for breaking down.

This was the yawn of time while a murder
Awaited another murder. I did not see
My father's murder, but I see it now always around me,
And I see it shapeless : as when we are sometimes told
Of the heroes who walk out into the snow and blizzard
To spare their comrades care, we always see
A white direction in which the figure goes,
And a vague ravine in which he stumbles and falls.
My father rises thus from a bath of blood,
Groping from table to chair in a dusky room
Through doorways into darkening corridors,
Falling at last in the howling vestibule.

In the years that followed, the winds of time swept round
The anniversaries of the act ; and they
Were shouted down : my mother prepared for them
Music and dance, and called them celebrations.
They did not, fever-laden, creep on her unaware.
But did the nights not turn on her ? Did she not
Dream music in the false-dawn faltering, phrases
Repeating endlessly, a figure of the dance
Halting and beckoning ?

It is my house now, decaying but never dying,
The soul's museum, preserving and embalming
The shuttered rooms, the amulets, the pictures,
The doorways waiting for perennial surprises,
The children sleeping under the heat of summer,
And lastly the great bronze doors of the bridal chamber,
Huge and unspeaking, not to be pressed and opened,
Not to be lingered near, then or thereafter,
Not to be pounded upon by desolate fists,
Mine least of all.
                        I sailed with dipping sails.
I was not guilty of anybody's blood.
I will protect them in the decaying house.

With this resolve, concluded like a prayer,
From the eyes of the window gently stealing away,

As in a ritual I wipe the dust from the mirror
And look through the dark at the dim reflection before me.
The lips draw back from the mouth,
The night draws back from the years,
And there is the family smile in the quivering room.

The sun has gone, and the hunted bird demands :
' *Can the liar guard the truth, the deceiver seek it,*
The murderer preserve, the harlot chasten, or the guilty
Shelter the innocent ? And shall you protect ? '

Henry Reed.

BATHERS

THEY flutter out of white, and run
through the electric wind to bathe,
giggling like rivers for the fun
of smacking mud in the toes, of lithe
and sliding bodies like their own
—sharp rushes, good to battle with.

The child knows all delight to be
naked and queer as his own name,
foreign as being loved : but he
feels as a kind of coming home
the flags that slap his plunging knee,
and the cold stocking of the stream.

Coiling in wombs of water, bent
backwards upon the sheets of air,
his wand of sexless body lent
to all that was or casts before,
he strips to either element
a foetus or a ravisher.

So gladly virgin rivers rush
down to their amniotic seas,
children of cold and glittering flesh
that promise harvest as they pass
panics of tiny fertile fish
in the fast pale of boisterous thighs.

Terence Tiller.

BROTHER FIRE

WHEN our brother Fire was having his dog's day
Jumping the London streets with millions of tin cans
Clanking at his tail, we heard some shadow say
' Give the dog a bone '—and so we gave him ours ;
Night after night we watched him slaver and crunch away
The beams of human life, the tops of topless towers.

Which gluttony of his for us was Lenten fare
Who mother-naked, suckled with sparks, were chill
Though dandled on a grid of sizzling air
Striped like a convict—black, yellow and red ;
Thus were we weaned to knowledge of the Will
That wills the natural world but wills us dead.

O delicate walker, babbler, dialectician Fire,
O enemy and image of ourselves,
Did we not on those mornings after the All Clear,
When you were looting shops in elemental joy
And singing as you swarmed up city block and spire,
Echo your thoughts in ours ? ' Destroy! Destroy! '

Louis MacNeice.

[89]

SPRINGBOARD

He never made the dive—not while I watched.
High above London, naked in the night
Perched on a board. I peered up through the bars
Made by his fear and mine but it was more than fright
That kept him crucified among the budding stars.

Yes, it was unbelief. He knew only too well
That circumstances called for sacrifice
But, shivering there, spreadeagled above the town,
His blood began to haggle over the price
History would pay if he were to throw himself down.

If it would mend the world, that would be worth while
But he, quite rightly, long had ceased to believe
In any Utopia or in Peace-upon-Earth ;
His friends would find in his death neither ransom nor reprieve
But only a grain of faith—for what it was worth.

And yet we know he knows what he must do.
There above London where the gargoyles grin
He will dive like a bomber past the broken steeple,
One man wiping out his own original sin
And, like ten million others, dying for the people.

Louis MacNeice.

ABEL

My brother Cain, the wounded, liked to sit
Brushing my shoulder, by the staring water
Of life, or death, in cinemas half-lit
By scenes of peace that always turned to slaughter.

He liked to talk to me. His eager voice
Whispered the puzzle of his bleeding thirst,
Or prayed me not to make my final choice,
Unless we had a chat about it first.

And then he chose the final pain for me.
I do not blame his nature : he's my brother ;
Nor what you call the times : our love was free,
Would be the same at any time ; but rather

The ageless ambiguity of things
Which makes our life mean death, our love be hate.
My blood that streams across the bedroom sings :
' I am my brother opening the gate! '

Demetrios Capetanakis.

SEEN FROM THE OPEN WINDOW

SEEN from the open window
The lonely vistas widen ;
The mind invents its thunder
While innocence in wonder
Looks for the pure horizon.

Though what the bird may offer
Can teach the mind to suffer,
Only the bone will enter
And with the knife of Winter
Skate frozen water.

Surely the mind may fathom
The pyramid and column,

But not that single fibre
Whose dark unearthly fever
Divides the world for ever.

Peter Yates.

A LANDSCAPE

THIS would have made a poem
When I was younger,
The mountain road, the larches,
At the farm called The Finger.

Now there is nothing to write about
In a morning heavy with thunder,
The wind rifling the corn,
And the savage and tender
Green of the mustard field,
The black plantation
Of firs in the round valley,
And the wind suddenly dying
At the back of a cloud,
While the hot smell of the earth
Oppresses the nostrils,
And the birds falling
Instantly silent
Leave a dove still calling
Down below in the woods ;
Up here in the hills the thunder
Ruminates from one to the other.

Perhaps when I was younger
Some kind of addition
Could have made this a round number ;
Now I only need to remember,

Faithfully, this shadow on summer,
And the silence made in the mountains
By the dove and the thunder.

Joan Barton.

ASKARI'S SONG

At dusk when the sky is pale
Across a three years' journey
I can see the far white hill
Which in my land is like a
Conscience or maker.

At dusk when cattle cross
The red dust of the roadway,
I smell the sweetish grass,
Half animal, half flowers,
Which also is ours.

At dusk the roads along
The separating plains are
So sad with our deep song
I could expect the mountain
To drift like a fountain,

And, conquering time, our tribe
Out of the dust to meet us
Come happy, free, alive,
Bringing the snow-capped boulder
Over their shoulder.

Roy Fuller.

WAITING FOR SPRING, 1943

A grey wind blows
Through the woods, and the birches are bare,
And the hazel crooks its catkins tight as a starling's claws;
But out in the fields where the dyker hacks the branches
Of purple willow and elder and wrenches
The trunks square to the run of the hedge, there
The yellow lamb's-tails dangle in the frosty air.

So also we
On the perimeter and fringe of war,
Open to the sunlight and the wind from the western sea,
Wounded by the knife of winter, still
Feel the bright blood rise to bear
White and daring blossoms, fledged before
The seabirds leave the ploughland or the snow leaves the fell.

Let us not forget
Those in whom autumn dug deep furrows of pain,
Those to whom winter has been the kindliest season yet,
The snow their only eiderdown, the frost
Their only morphia; they will not greet again
The sap that stings in the bone, nor the bird on the nest
That hatches globes of suffering in the probing rain.

Blood flows back
Into the frozen hand with pain,
And children whimper as the wind flogs them again awake.
To those defeated by the winter's cold
Spring is a terrible season, atonement not to be told
To us in our temperate valleys, who scarcely have begun
To feel the anger of love beneath the conquering sun.

Norman Nicholson.

INVOCATION

STAR of eternal possibles and joy,
Vibrate the marble with your kiss!
On ancient columns and dark walls
     Fall with unearthly calls,
Bird-supple wings disturbing air!

Fall like the rain on praying hands;
Bring to the living-haunted hills
Remote perspectives and new worlds—
     Invasion of the wilds,
Illumination of nocturnal fairs!

Disturb the logic of bleak winds—
Rotations of the mind unwinding life;
And in the midnight waiting groves,
     The ever-talking graves
Crying aloud the perfect word.

Aim for the fringe, the thinnest curve
Where strength of possible despairs;
The missing but imagined arc
     For which the circle aches,
The vista waiting to be seen.

I breaking from the ring of we,
Cries in its isolation still:
A leap from sequence into void!
     But in that daring vague
The ether challenges with form.

O star of mind's dark inwardness,
Prolong the struggle with your force!
By your not-being dare to be
     More than the eye can see,
A silence audible with growth.

Peter Yates.

THE WALL

THE place where our two gardens meet
Is undivided by a street,
And mingled flower and weed caress
And fill our double wilderness,
Among whose riot undismayed
And unreproached, we idly played,
While, unaccompanied by fears,
The months extended into years,
Till we went down one day in June
To pass the usual afternoon
And there discovered, shoulder-tall,
Rise in the wilderness a wall :
The wall which put us out of reach
And into silence split our speech.
We knew, and we had always known
That some dark, unseen hand of stone
Hovered across our days of ease,
And strummed its tunes upon the breeze.
It had not tried us overmuch,
But here it was, for us to touch.

The wilderness is still as wild,
And separately unreconciled
The tangled thickets play and sprawl
Beneath the shadows of our wall,
And the wall varies with the flowers
And has its seasons and its hours.
Look at its features wintrily
Frozen to transparency ;
Through it an icy music swells
And a brittle, brilliant chime of bells :
Would you conjecture that, in Spring,
We lean upon it, talk and sing,
Or climb upon it, and play chess
Upon its summer silentness ?

One certain thing alone we know :
Silence or song, it does not go.
A habit now to wake with day
And watch it catch the sun's first ray,
Or terrorised to scramble through
The depths of night to prove it true.

We need not doubt, for such a wall
Is based in death, and does not fall.

Henry Reed.

ELEGY

TREE of the hillside, Apple tree,
high in the morning
drop your red apples.

The shadows of birds and their small bright mouths
leap over woods that part the bending rivers—
over the creeping ridges, valley to valley
the spires of cockcrow and the cold bell answer
far to the blind sea, to the drowned ledges ;
spanned by the sky's wide beaches. Or fine spires
the gold birds flash swinging above the copses
and out of farms under the intricate sky
the tall necks yell incessant at the morning—

among your leaves of the fountain
a hundred reddening globes, the faces of children
tree of the chalk hill, apple tree
roll your red apples to the parishes ;
down to wet valleys, by streams, hung with the leaves' old faces.

The faces of birds clash on the sharp beaks of the dead.
Those leaping spears that drive the graveyards home
into the spongy hills, restore the pattern
of crops and the order of fields, and the roads run over
the road-builders, and the quilts of corn
cover cold farmers. But the sharp sad faces
the skulls of killed sheep, the staring cups
robbed long of gold and bitter eyes
lie in white outposts on the hills' brown lid.
Hollow stones, scattered in windy places
on the high moors, no spire or cockcrow reaches.

Tree of the hillside, Apple tree
whom no lid deceives, whose slim roots wander
the brown cells of the hill, caressed
by hard, quick fingers that have forgotten apples
that have forgotten the skill of the harrow, the old
skill of the crooked roads and the flight of herons
that have forgotten the long and bitter barrow
cast your bright faces, children's sorrowless faces.

O poet, hillside tree, O swift combiner
of the sad hunters' messages tapped in the dark hill
into the upgoing song of leaves and the red
cold falling faces of your pure children
fountain voice, taught by the voiceless faces
show me your knowledge—cast your happy fruit.

The cocks ride swinging, over the brown male voices :
but always under the fields, battened and locked
grey mouths instruct me that have forgotten lips—
the hatches move as I walk over them,
always the beggars, the bereft, through the bars of the fields
call me, plead for my voice, for my voice, to borrow it,
and I am dumb to fling the mumbled sign
the glimpsed deep woods, the sound of tusk and horn
and the long arrow flying down the years
up to the deep sky, into the singing fountain.

O apple tree
O green interpreter
distil this tossing sorrow
into your red timeless apples . . .

Now after cockcrow on the populous hills
we stand between the living and the sharp
beseeching faces, pressing from the earth
their urchin heads to the cloudy panes of the grass
apple tree, upright speaker, deliverer
of these red perfect warnings, give me your courage.
When I am silent, I can hear the teeth
gnash in the blind hill. I am ambassador
unwilling of so many. Teach me to live
a speaking fountain for the tongueless faces.

Teach me acceptance.
I did not choose them
Even in childhood there were hands that plucked at my feet.

Apple tree, tree of the hillside
down on the riding spires, for tears
toss your red apples.

Alex Comfort.

THE OLD MILL

THE water rushes under the house,
The water fills every room and the walled garden—
Or gardens, for walls and hedges and surprises are many—
With cold monotonous roar,
Slides under a low green tunnel
To the wide, foaming pool below
Where old men fish from the bridge.

[99]

Beyond the garden the river flows
Straight between the meadows clumped with elms ;
To bless your evening, there is sunset behind the elms.
Narrow wooden bridge joins the divided garden ;
Slanting, half across the river runs
Comb-like bar to catch weed and wood ;
In winter, you say, enough driftwood
Mounts against the bar for fires.
Like all who enter this house we lean over the bridge
And talk and watch—as safety valve—what is in the water,
In the water heavy and slow before the bar and fall,
Tentacular weed, little fish above the mud by bank,
Dark pool and light, stick and leaf.
Married, you have lived here just two years.
Intelligent and rapidly superficial—as you used to be—
You talk of garden and house. Of nothing else.
You grow aubergines and peppers and pumpkins,
Your husband and you put up the greenhouse,
Shoes go mouldy everywhere with damp
That eats through the walls, you go to bed
Early and get up early, apples kept well
Last year because you waited, picking
At the right moment instead of hastily picking
What was left after great winds stole the crop.
Hungrily, with your long fingers, you enjoy your senses,
And yet these things you grow do not live.
A chill, like chill of the metallic slide of water,
Exudes out of this life you build.
All day long what is your root-hair life ? Really what do you feel
As you glory in this sunset over the meadows ?
As you watch the water, standing on the bridge,
Resting after housework,—for as you tell me
You have no servants—what do you see besides the weed ?
In the one-leaf cyclamen seedling, growing for next spring,
What touches you ? Sometimes cold agony of emptiness ?
The water eats away, slowly the water surges. The house will topple.

In the ruins, in the water and stone, how will you stand ?

Under the aubergine leaf, in the apple boughs there sighs
A death. Does this, not the damp river air, make you tired ?
Under the aubergine leaf there sighs an end.
Under the aubergine leaf there sighs a promise,
But not made by you. Living things will live,
And man with woman not live on an island in the water.
Living things will live, another river press.

Theresa Ashton.

BRING BACK

Salt sea, sweet sea,
Sail my lover back to me.

Then will winters lose their sting,
The dumb sorrow depart from spring ;
I shall rise early in the morning ;
The endless afternoons shall bring
No sick weariness to me ;
I shall be beautiful and free.

I shall not hate the baby's crying—
I shall hear the turtle sing.
Taste shall equal scent ; rejoicing
Really be now, not past or coming ;
Having outdo desire, and longing
Lead to delight ; my poetry
Come out as it was meant to be.
Then to be good will be easy.

If he returns across the sea
Shall all these mercies really be ?

Shall we see raindrops upward rain
Figs grow on thorns, and an end of pain,
Because your lover comes again ?

Affluent hearts have power through
Their alembic to make life new—
But likelier life goes on as before.
Love can do all, but needs more
Than fortune and a rapturous hour.
Tedious and rare tasks are done
Ere rivers run dry and rocks melt with the sun.

Anne Ridler.

A LATE ACQUAINTANCE

His heart was carefree
That's not much to say
Of a young man. All have that touch
An excited way. Whatever
He might clutch, it showed him clever,
That was his amusing pose,
Clown in clover.

Heigho! Why should we wonder
At the young bounder
Now he is some feet under ?
Our thoughts cannot make fonder
The earth that's his last plunder,
Nor can regret impose
Peace where he goes.

Lawrence Little.

A TRANCE

Her love, enclosed in lineaments of grace,
Which is my care, as my love is her care,
Burns through us when we kiss

—The sapphire in the rose of the embrace.
Her loving virtue witnesses
The love in me, which it saved from despair,
Under the care of her caress.

Sometimes, apart in sleep, by chance,
She falls out of my care alone,
Into the chaos of a trance.
I see a cloud move through the sunset bone
Of her familiar head, and, torn
Across the petals of her mouth, is shown
The slumbering path left by a thorn.

Restless, she turns to me, and presses
Those timid words against my ear
Which thunder at my heart like stones.
'Mercy,' she murmurs, and asks ' Who blesses ? '
Or ' I am pursued by time,' she moans.
I watch that precipice of fear
She treads, among her naked distresses.

To that deep care we are committed
Beneath the forests of our flesh
And shuddering scenery of these dreams,
Where unmasked agony is permitted
And bones are bared of flesh that seems ;
Our hands, unravelling beauty's mesh,
Meet our real selves, our charms outwitted.

Her pure trance is the oracle
Which speaks no language but the heart.
Our angel with our devil meets,
In the atrocious night, nor do they part,
But each forgives and greets,
And their mutual terrors heal
Within our love's deep miracle.

                                        Stephen Spender.

MILKMAID

THE girl's far treble, muted to the heat,
calls like a fainting bird across the fields
to where her flock lies panting for her voice,
their black horns buried deep in marigolds.

They climb awake, like drowsy butterflies,
and press their red flanks through the tall branched grass,
and as they go their wandering tongues embrace
the vacant summer mirrored in their eyes.

Led to the limestone shadows of a barn
they snuff their past embalmèd in the hay,
while her cool hand, cupped to the udder's fount,
distils the brimming harvest of their day.

Look what a cloudy cream the earth gives out,
fat juice of buttercups and meadow-rye ;
the girl dreams milk within her body's field
and hears, far off, her muted children cry.

Laurie Lee.

THE LILACS AND THE ROSES

O MONTHS of blossoming, months of transfigurations,
May without a cloud and June stabbed to the heart,
I shall not ever forget the lilacs or the roses
Nor those the Spring has kept folded away apart.

I shall not ever forget the tragic sleight-of-hand,
The cavalcade, the cries, the crowd, the sun,
The lorries loaded with love, the Belgian gifts,
The road humming with bees, the atmosphere that spun,

[104]

The feckless triumphing before the battle,
The scarlet blood the scarlet kiss bespoke
And those about to die bolt upright in the turrets
Smothered in lilac by a drunken folk.

I shall not ever forget the flower-gardens of France—
Illuminated scrolls from eras more than spent—
Nor forget the trouble of dusk, the sphinx-like silence,
The roses all along the way we went;
Flowers that gave the lie to the soldiers passing
On wings of fear, a fear importunate as a breeze,
And gave the lie to the lunatic push-bikes and the ironic
Guns and the sorry rig of the refugees.

But what I do not know is why this whirl
Of memories always comes to the same point and drops
At Sainte-Marthe . . . a general . . . a black pattern . . .
A Norman villa where the forest stops;
All is quiet here, the enemy rests in the night
And Paris has surrendered, so we have just heard—
I shall never forget the lilacs nor the roses
Nor those two loves whose loss we have incurred;

Bouquets of the first day, lilacs, Flanders lilacs,
Soft cheek of shadow rouged by death—and you,
Bouquets of the Retreat, delicate roses, tinted
Like far-off conflagrations: roses of Anjou.

Louis Aragon.

(*Translated from the French by* LOUIS MACNEICE.)

THE UNOCCUPIED ZONE

CROSS-FADE of grief to nothingness,
The beat of the crushed heart grew less,

The coals grew white and lost their gleam ;
Drinking the wine of summer's haze
In a rose-castle in Corrèze
I changed this August into dream.

What could it be that of a sudden
Brought an aching sob in the garden,
A voice of low reproach in the air ?
Ah not so soon, ah do not wake me ;
This merest snatch of song must take me
Out of the barracks of despair.

I thought for a moment that I heard
In the middle of the corn a blurred
Noise of arms—a theme that sears.
Whence did this theme return to me ?
Not carnations nor rosemary
Had thus retained the scent of tears.

By hook or crook I had got relief
From the dark secret of my grief
When lo—the shadows redivide ;
My eyes were only on the track
Of apathy that looks not back
When September dawned outside.

My love within your arms I lay
When someone hummed across the way
An ancient song of France ; my illness
At last came clear to me for good—
That phase of song like a naked foot
Rippled the green water of stillness.

Louis Aragon.

(*Translated from the French by* Louis MacNeice.)

WHAT IS TERRIBLE

LIFE at last I know is terrible :
The innocent scene, the innocent walls and light
And hills for me are like the cavities
Of surgery or dreams. The visible might
Vanish, for all it reassures, in white.

This apprehension has come slowly to me,
Like symptoms and bulletins of sickness. I
Must first be moved across two oceans, then
Bored, systematically and sickeningly,
In a place where war is news. And constantly

I must be threatened with what is certainly worse :
Peril and death, but no less boring. And
What else ? Besides my fear, my misspent time,
My love, hurt and postponed, there is the hand
Moving the empty glove ; the bland

Aspect of nothing disguised as something ; that
Part of living incommunicable,
For which we try to find vague adequate
Images, and which, after all,
Is quite surprisingly communicable.

Because in the clear hard light of war the ghosts
Are seen to be suspended by wires, and in
The old house the attic is empty : and the furious
Inner existence of objects and even
Ourselves is largely a myth : and for the sin

To blame our fathers, to attribute vengeance
To the pursuing chorus, and to live
In a good and tenuous world of private values,
Is simply to lie when only truth can give
Continuation in time to bread and love.

For what is terrible is the obvious
Organization of life : the oiled black gun,
And what it cost, the destruction of Europe by
Its councils ; the unending justification
Of that which cannot be justified, what is done.

The year, the month, the day, the minute, at war
Is terrible and my participation
And that of all the world is terrible.
My living now must bear the laceration
Of the herd, and always will. What's done

To me is done to many. I can see
No ghosts, but only the fearful actual
Lives of my comrades. If the empty whitish
Horror is ever to be flushed and real,
It must be for them and changed by them all.

Roy Fuller.

THE PERSIAN VERSION

TRUTH-LOVING Persians do not dwell upon
The trivial skirmish fought near Marathon.
As for the Greek theatrical tradition
Which represents that summer's expedition
Not as a mere reconnaissance in force
By three brigades of foot and one of horse
(Their left flank covered by some obsolete
Light craft detached from the main Persian fleet)
But as a grandiose, ill-starred attempt
To conquer Greece—they treat it with contempt ;
And only incidentally refute
Major Greek claims, by stressing what repute

The Persian monarch and the Persian nation
Won by this salutary demonstration:
Despite a strong defence and adverse weather
All arms combined magnificently together.

Robert Graves.

THE OLDEST SOLDIER

THE sun shines warm on seven old soldiers
    Paraded in a row,
Perched like starlings on the railings—
    Give them plug-tobacco!

They'll croon you the Oldest-Soldier Song,
    Of Harry who took a holiday
From the sweat of ever thinking for himself
    Or going his own bloody way.

It was arms-drill, guard and kit-inspection,
    Like dreams of a long train-journey,
And the barrack-bed that Harry dossed on
    Went rockabye, rockabye, rockabye.

Harry kept his rifle and brasses clean,
    But Jesus Christ, what a liar!
He won the Military Medal
    For his coolness under fire.

He was never the last on parade
    Nor the first to volunteer,
And when Harry rose to be storeman
    He seldom had to pay for his beer.

Twenty-one years, and out Harry came
    To be odd-job man, or janitor,
Or commissionaire at a picture-house,
    Or, some say, bully to a whore.

But his King and Country calling Harry,
    He reported again at the Depot,
To perch on this railing like a starling,
    The oldest soldier in the row.

                                    Robert Graves.

THE MOTIONLESS DANCER

TURNING from movement to sky
Accepting the wind and the lime,
A statue resting in time
Singes the living with thought.
Loving the fleshless and pure,
How muscular limbs endure
Like thresholds tempting the eye !

A feather descending the air,
Bruising the loneliest nerve ;
Insisting duration's curve
In menace of growing space!
See how they linger and burn,
Too wildly living to learn
His poise on the highest stair.

Watching the movement of birds,
The tear and the falling leaf,
The frictional force of life
Renewing the earth with green ;
Can living interpret his face ?
Apollo's immobile grace
Dividing the Word into words ?

Tempting the mind with the eyes,
Unfolding their form like shrouds,

The restless flowering clouds
Deride the thought which is still ;
But whispering blood remains
In the hairy ropes and stains
Where the ivy clasps his thighs.

In thought he has always been :
His pure and motionless force,
Like dying without remorse,
Troubles the living with calm ;
For balancing loving and grief,
He masters the daring leaf
Which brushes his lips with green.

Ask is he living or dead,
This god in durable stone ;
Himself the ultimate bone
Which sings in the flesh of all.
Calling the new and the strange,
The winds of eternal change
Circle his arrogant head.

Is he the labour and end,
The final of mind's resource—
This cold detachable force
Like pain in a frozen tear ?
Slowly the spirit may climb ;
He rests forever in time.
Knowing the will must bend.

Movement encircles his base.
Is it for living they strive ?
This bitter creative drive,
Lifting the blood out of flesh,
Cooling its danger with thought ?
For only the act is caught
In the sorrow that haunts his face.

Column surmounting the verge,
Lifting his head into sky!
While craving the movements die
He bridges the gulfs of life,
Moulding the ashes with form ;
Calm at the centre of storm,
His effortless ease the urge.

Living uncovers the lie
Of the restless moving waves,
And the wind whose veering saves
With its lovely voice of change.
In the forests ancient groan,
His pure symmetrical stone
Teaches the living to die.

Rivers unwinding their source,
Splinter the valleys with light,
Claiming that movement is right,
And the pure duration life.
See how the water's flowing
Prolongs its glitter of going,
Tempting the mind on its course !

And daily the baffling sea,
Exerting its ageless change ;
Proclaiming the far and strange
Expanding nature of world ;
Tempting the blood as it sings,
A tremor of vibrant wings
In the carnal rose to be.

Invisible rivets bind
His powerful upward urge
As his shoulders touch the verge
Of horizon's shadeless line.
Living may throb at his base,
But never define that face
Which beckons the daring mind.

Skirting the fringe they move
Like frail articulate birds,
Lovers creating their words
To arrest the darkening flood.
Calm on their wave of desire,
The fingers playing with fire
Deny what living will prove.

But calm which loving has left
Breathes out of the lonely bone
The candour which gives the stone
Its secret of living death ;
Bursting the prison of sense
His being is made intense,
And lives by living bereft.

A passion without desire—
Who in these genitive storms
Deciphers in ancient forms
The truth of its dazzling nil ?
Will ever the strong and live,
Who accept and proudly strive
Acclaim its terrible fire ?

Though watching a falling leaf,
The blood may long to be still ;
The hesitant human will
Divides the source of its calm :
Charmed by the glitter of act,
Living can never retract
The passionate taint of life.

Brushing the foam of the clouds,
Releasing an inward storm,
His pure symbolical form
Stands over the curving world.
Dying interprets his face ;
Still its inflexible grace
Propels the shivering crowds.

Is ever his secret caught,
Resolved in the mind and known;
Desired for joy alone?
Imagined and motionless dance;
Centre of mobile storm—
His is the ultimate form
The flesh into Word has thought!

Piercing the tremulous heart;
Deriding the natural laws;
Asserting himself the cause
Of all that ever remains;
This force which nothing can kill:
A glimpse of his haunting nil
In delicate bones and art.

                                        Peter Yates.

DOWN ON THE DELTA

It's a watery world down on the delta below
New Orleans where the tourists never go,
Land rich as black gold that the giant river
Has stolen from America, old thief, great giver,
Who brings Kansas, Illinois, Louisiana as a present
To that ocean woman for whom they were not meant,
Creates a tropic tongue under a Flemish sky
Where marshes drip with hyacinth and egrets fly,
A thick explosion of life from the dripping mud—
The river surges through it like a placid god;
Unseen behind the dykes, unseen but near, it shakes
The roots of the small houses and sometimes wakes
Millions of wild geese where the lighted liner passes
Sending a rush of wings up from the shaken grasses,
A god who feeds the plump sleek otter and the hunter,
The trees of golden apples and the anxious planter

Who pays the nigger children to crack whips
Over the greedy rice-devouring crows—a land of ships,
Where the wild fishermen can take their 'cajun' gals,
And drink their liquor up and play the slot-machines,
It is a land of great skies and of tropic greens.

But the birds have French names and this is the queer thing
That in the night a song your mother used to sing
May sound out of the darkness and make you weep,
'Au clair de la lune' or the one about the sheep,
And now in evil days for France a bird called 'Tricolore',
One saying 'Prier Dieu' over and over again, is more
French than anything in France, and O the 'Rouge Moqueur'
Can shriek his anger here upon the lonely air.

                                        May Sarton.
                                        (U.S.A.)

COLLIERY COUNTRY

WE said the country started at the brook.
At least the houses ended, and the sodden
Meadows bore other crop than scaffold-poles
Brick-heaps and drain-pipes. It was country of a sort.
We looked for coltsfoot in the boggy fields and angled
The minnows that darted round the sardine cans
Under the shot-silk surface film of oil;
And ran through the colliery village with held breath
Because the colliers and the colliers' children
Spoke with strange accents and had black faces.

But that was when we were little. Afterwards,
In fog, in rain, in the teeth of the new-broom gale,
Night after night I hunted this colliery country
Seeking for something. I could not give it a name
But sometimes almost found it:

                            when a banjo strummed

And men sang boozily in the Colliers' Arms ;
Or when a goods train rattled through the cutting,
Its ruddy steam, mist-tangled, the blown-back
Hair of a giant girl ; or when,
After the dazzling lights of a car rushed by
And darkness shuttered down like a hen's wing,
I was alone in darkness and against
My own heart's beat could only hear the regular
Heavy monotonous beat of the colliery pump.
And, for the time it takes a match to burn out,
The pump was the heart's thump of the tilting earth
And earth a sleeping animal that would wake
One day ; the whale that Sinbad walked ; and I
Sinbad the parasite. In all that darkness,
There was only
The pumping heart and that great threshing stroke.
Trembling with too-great terror, I awaited
The reassurance of nocturnal noises,
Dogs barking, trains, and wind-borne human voices ;
Anything but that inhuman alien heart.

I knew as well as now, it was just a pump ;
But did not see why it should not be both.

                                        Walter Allen.

PRAGUE DRESSED IN LIGHT

I walked in the late dusk one day
—Then Prague seemed lovelier than Rome—
This dream would never pass away
I thought, and I not wake, when come
Stars from their daylight place of hiding
The winged, armed gargoyle, whose dark form is

Under the old cathedral cornice
Like a sentinel protruding.

One day I walked in the first dawn
(I thought it useless to sleep more)
The bolt of the great gate was drawn
I was afraid to knock the door.
Alas, the pilgrim waits outside
The spring morning with no key!
The gargoyle I had wished to see
At dawn, when the stars cease to hide.

But I saw a grave; and I went to it:
Being alone, I had no fears.
Like a wreck was the dead man's shoe: its
Tip was pointing towards the stars.
Above the sleeping brow, when the flame
Trembled, I saw the shadow steal.
And I could hear the spinning wheel
And, from the vineyard, singing came.

We wove in the mantle of the king
Grapes gray as human breath at dawn.
In the nave, four ladies sleeping
The dead one on their breasts have borne.
Greet the woods round Castle Tyn
Falling gently into the plain
O greet that Karluv Tyn again
And the hillsides flowing with wine.

From his deep grave, he raised above
The pillars grown under his palm,
A white skull: made only for love
His hands which loved it were a balm.
It was made sacred by the song
Of the people, with parched lips;
It strengthened him, a charm that slips
From the great heirloom wrecked so long.

How could his lips do else than parch ?
Ceaselessly on a sword he slept.
For ages past the chorale march
With ardent watch his surety kept.
The saint is covered with the wings
Of angels, and a shield of prayer.
He broke white bread which the poor share
And crushed grapes with his feet, a king's.

Dazed near the Majesty so great,
Towards the beggars' doors I creep.
I did not come to weep into the agate,
The time had passed when I could weep.
A broken stand opens the music.
Someone has torn the embroidered altar.
The heels of boots, without falter,
Hollow on the gold mosaics, click.

Jaroslav Seifert.

(Translated from the Czech by STEPHEN SPENDER
and JIŘI MUCHA).

ONE DAY IN SPRING

GONE is the winter's cold
In the wild wood and the heart—
And warm are the young leaves and the budding spray.
' O heart, O eyes, O lips that will grow not old,
The waters love the moon, the sun the day,
As I love you, my day's darling ! '

Said the youth of the world. But a living dead man walked
In the spring fire and talked
As if one heard him—though in all the spring
No heart was listening.

(' O heed him not, my dew with golden feet
Flying from me, my dew that is born of the spring heat.')

' On that last day she said " I shall be cold
To the world's end without your kiss . . . But when Death is so old
He no more feels the pain
Of jealous love, I shall be yours again.

' " On that great holiday
There'll be no work, no fear for to-morrow's bread
Nor will the nations rage—
And only Death will know the sorrow of old age."

' Then, Sun of my life, she went to warm the Dead,
And I must go now sunless in their stead.

' I felt not the cold wind blow—
No the change of the sun :
For earth and sea
And my heart were one :
Where nothing grew ; they nothing knew
Except the world was done.

' They clothed a dead man in my dress
Who rose in the morning sorrow
And all day walked the world, waving at Nothingness
—Now high, now low,
Changing with every wind like a scarecrow.

' Sometimes my voice would sound from those dead lips :
For I who had seen
Each stain of age, fatigue upon her cheek—
Dimming her beauty—I who had feared to see
That eternal truth the Bone
Laid bare by Death—cried now, " Come home! Whatever stain
Death laid upon you, in whatever guise
You are now, I should know your heart!
                    Come home, out of the rain,

' " The cold! How shall I bear my heart without its beat,
My clay without its soul ? . . . I am alone—
More cold than you are in your grave's long night
That has my heart for covering, warmth and light."

' The cathedrals and their creeds were built above
Her heart, and all the Babels of the world,
Their bells and madness tolled " Dead " over her love. . . .
But the earth and all the roots of trees in the winter earth
Yet could not hold her down—
The tides of seas and seasons could not drown

' Her heart . . . So after twelve months in her grave
She came to me and gave
Her kiss . . . humbly and pleadingly she crept beside
My bed and looked at me with those hollow eyes
That seemed as if they had wept
For the stains Death left upon her beauty, fearing I might
Love her no more—so she came home from her endless night

' And the lips of my dead love were warm to me.
But the lips, the heart, should be dust-dun, death-cold
From that long night . . . and so I feared to hold
That heart that came warm from the grave . . . Afraid
Of that eternity of love, I laid
Death's earth upon her heart : for this
Dead man in my dress dared not kiss
Her who laid by Death's cold lest I
Should feel it when she came to lie
Upon my heart . . . my dead love gave
Lips warm with love through from her grave—
And I gave Death her love—the only light
And fire she had to warm her eternal night.'

So he went by . . . and as the snowflake's star can see
Its ephemeral cold in the eternity

Of the rock crystal's six rays—, so light grief and waterfalls
See that eternal grief that melts not though the last spring calls

The heart . . .
        But where the wild birds sing
We walked together
And pitied the poor Dead for whom the spring
Is cold, for all the strange green fire
In eyes, on hair—the world, the veins, changed into emeralds.

O Dead, your heart is gone! you cannot weep,
And like the unborn child's should be your sleep

But on your lips, long worn away, a youthful smile
Remains, a thing of sorrow—

And wasted so thin by hopeless love you seem a shade—
An echo only—

You wait for one who comes not, for the hour
When your lips spoke and winter broke in flower,

The Parthenon was built by your dead kiss . . .
What should love seek now you are changed to this

Thin piteous wreck—yet strong as the Prophet's rock :
No grief tears waters from that stone to mock

Death's immobility—and changed to stone
Those eyelids see one sight, and one alone.

What do they see ? Some lost and childish kiss
In summer, in the dews of a dead morning—
The meeting, and clasp of hands, the last farewell
Among the morning sorrows ? Now in spring

Beneath the young green-blooming strawberry
In the deep groves they sigh for the forgotten bliss
—Grown dead and rotten, of their lover's kiss,
Forgetting the young heart grows old
And in the Spring night they must sleep alone.[1]

        [1] *Note : An adaptation from a line by Sappho.*

But in the spring warmth creatures, faiths and men
Awaken in the sun—
The coldness of the heart
Is with the winter done—

And the waters love the moon, the sun the day
As I love my day's darling.—

Though all the lovers of the world
Grow old, and fade, and die—
Yet how should you and I ?
For the world was only made that we should love—
O heart, O eyes, O lips that will never grow old.

Edith Sitwell.

SCHIZOPHRENE

HEARING off-stage the taps filling the bath
The set dissolves to childhood—in her cot
Hearing that ominous relentless noise
Which the grown-ups have started, who are not
She knows, aware of what it means ; it means
The Dark, the Flood, the Malice. It destroys
All other meanings—dolls or gingerbread ;
It means a Will that wills all children dead.

Hearing the gas fire breathe monotonously
She waits for words but no words come, she lifts
A soapstone hand to smoothe her hair and feels
The hand is someone else's—the scene shifts
To a cold desert where the wind has dropped
And the earth's movement stopped and something steals
Up from the grit through nerve and bone and vein
To flaunt its iron tendrils in her brain.

Hearing again the telegraph wires again
Humming again and always, she must lean
Against the humming post and search her mind
For what it is they say; in some latrine
She knows she wrote it first upon the wall
In self-incrimination, duly signed;
And, unrevoked since then, that signature
Runs round the world on wires, accusing her.

Hearing the church-bells, too, she knows at once
That only she can hear them for it is no
Church or even belfry where they hang,
There are no ropes attached or ringers down below,
These bells are disembodied, they express
The claims of frozen chaos and will clang
Till this and every other world shall melt
And Chaos be Itself and nothing felt.

Lastly, hearing the cock in the grey dawn
Crow once, crow twice, she shivers and dissolves
To someone else who in the hour of trial
Denied his Master and his guilt devolves
On her head only. If she could speak up,
She might even now atone for that denial
But the grey cock still crows and she knows why;
For she must still deny, deny, deny.

Louis MacNeice.

THE PETTY OFFICERS' MESS

JUST now I visited the monkeys: they
Are captive near the mess. And so the day
Ends simply with a sudden darkness, while
Again across the palm trees, like a file,
          The rain swings from the bay.

The radio speaks, the lights attract the flies,
Above them and the rain our voices rise,
And somewhere from this hot and trivial place
As the news tells of death, with pleasant face,
                Comes that which is not lies.

The voices argue : *Soldiers in the end*
Turn scarecrows ; their ambiguous figures blend
With all who are obsessed by food and peace.
The rulers go, they cannot order these
                Who are not disciplined.

O cars with abdicating princes : streets
Of untidy crowds : O terrible defeats !
Such images which haunt us of the past
Flash on the present like the exile's vast
                Shivers and fleshy heats ;

But never coincide. Do they approach ?
Upon that doubt I'm frightened to encroach—
Show me, I say, *the organizations that*
Will change the rags and mob into the state,
                Like pumpkin into coach.

The voices make no answer. Music now
Throbs through the room and I remember how
The little pickaxe shapes of swallows swerve
From balconies and whitewashed walls ; a curve
                Of bird-blue bay ; a dhow :

Small stabbing observations! And I know
(The cheap song says it on the radio)
That nerves and skin first suffer when we part,
The deep insensitive tissues of the heart
                Later, when time is slow.

And time has done his part and stands and looks
With dumb exasperated face. The books

Year after year record the crisis and
The passion, but no change. The measuring sand
        Is still. There are no flukes,

Like the virtuous sulphonamides, to kill
The poisons of the age, but only will :
Reduction of desires to that cold plan
Of raping the ideal ; the new frail man
        Who slays what's in the hill.

The monkeys near the mess (where we all eat
And dream) I saw to-night select with neat
And brittle fingers dirty scraps, and fight,
And then look pensive in the fading light,
        And after pick their feet.

They are secured by straps about their slender
Waists, and the straps to chains. Most sad and tender,
They clasp each other and look round with eyes
Like ours at what their strange captivities
        Invisibly engender.

Roy Fuller.

EMILY DICKINSON

I STAND like a deserted church
That would much rather be
A garden with a hopping bird,
Or with a humming bee.

I did not want eternity,
I only begged for time :
In the trim head of chastity
The bells of madness chime.

Their song blows up a monstrous bee
With burning eyes and beard.
If bees don't look as big as God,
They look at least as weird.

My nights are haunted circuses
Where deadly freaks perform
The trick of stabbed eternity,
The triumph of the worm.

While in the fertile fields of love
Industrious farmers plod,
My days are brooding on man's doom,
The meaning of the rod.

But thought is vain. Man cannot find
What stupid monsters mean.
One night of wrath I closed my door
On God, and called him mean.

And so I lost Him for a bee ;
He lost me for a freak.
Ah, in the grip of boundlessness
The joints of reason creak.

I stand as boundless as a church
That has no door for God,
While in the fruitful fields of love
Ignorant farmers plod.

Demetrios Capetanakis.

FRAGMENT OF AN ELEGY

THERE are many dead in the brutish desert,
        who lie uneasy
among the scrub in this landscape of half-wit

stunted ill-will. For the dead land is insatiate
and necrophilous. The sand is blowing about still.
Many who for various reasons, or because
              of mere unanswerable compulsion, came here
and fought among the clutching gravestones,
              shivered and sweated,
cried out, suffered thirst, were stoically silent, cursed
the spittering machine-guns, were homesick for Europe
and fast embedded in quicksand of Africa
              agonized and died.
And sleep now. Sleep here the sleep of the dust.

There were our own, there were the others.
Their deaths were like their lives, human and animal.
There were no gods and precious few heroes.
What they regretted when they died had nothing to do with
              race and leader, realm indivisible,
laboured Augustan speeches or vague imperial heritage.
(They saw through that guff before the axe fell.)
              Their longing turned to
the lost world glimpsed in the memory of letters :
an evening at the pictures in the friendly dark,
two knowing conspirators smiling and whispering secrets ; or else
a family gathering in the homely kitchen
with Mum so proud of her boys in uniform :
              their thoughts trembled
between moments of estrangement, and ecstatic moments
of reconciliation : and their desire
crucified itself against the unutterable shadow of someone
whose photo was in their wallets.
Then death made his incision

There were our own, there were the others.
Therefore, minding the great word of Glencoe's
son, that we should not disfigure ourselves
with villainy of hatred ; and seeing that all
have gone down like curs into anonymous silence,
I will bear witness for I knew the others.

Seeing that littoral and interior are alike indifferent
And the birds are drawn again to our welcoming north
Why should I not sing *them*, the dead, the innocent?
Hamish Henderson.

MY PLATOON

MARCHING at ease against the fanning dust
Pleased with themselves and happy, whistle and sing
Their bawdy and their sentimental songs.

How thirty of them can, acting together,
Become one person, a Lancashire lad.
' —Oh she likes a little bit in the morning—'

Then break up for their intimate moments;
Listening to Vera Lynn, reading their letters.
' —I'll be with you in apple blossom time—'

Alone on sentry in the bomb smashed docks,
The movement in the ruined shadows beyond—
When you visit that silhouette against the phosphorescent sea
You get so near and get so very fond.
Bernard Gutteridge.

A POET KILLED IN ACTION

A MAN is a kind of alchemist
A heart a flaming crucible where
Meet and mingle these elements,
Passion and memory. And all
Sweet savours added, and gall.
Only unwelcome winds of death

Shall cool the fire; yet death's
Better alternative if you have time
For distillation, is power.

While you work through the long night
By a light in your lonely window
And await a new element, wondering,
Afraid there will not be time,
Half of your mind is open, unhurt,
Not furrowed or scarred, or
Senses revolted, heart suffocated
And you are revived from the poison
You will always already know.

But always was suddenly never;
And all the great dammed-up tears
For you, and all that were never yours
Burst into elegy over despairing lands
And, trembling no more, your hands
Touched the shimmering, wavy horizon,
Held it apart; while the sun burnt out.
Somebody crazy put out the light
And spoilt your experiment; this
Tiny explosion could not have shattered the world.

Death is no disguise but only death,
And now you are dead, memory's crinkled
And tears are salted with anger.

Antony Brown.

LEAVE TRAIN

YELLOW as flowers as dead fingers
yellow as death as a mandarin
dawn with eyes like a stranger
dawn with a handful of sick flowers.

The stumps of memory are broken trees
the stumps of memory are amputated fingers
the patient sick with ether
dreams unflowered avenues of anger.

Grief clenched like a fist, a
sprawled hand, grief pitted with shell:
the bell of the blood in a deep sea
drowns, the hood of the face is eyeless.

Dawn constellated with sick stars
dawn hedged round with smoke
yellow as fog as cornflowers
yellow as a dog as a deathshead.

Like dissevered arteries and veins
like brains cauterized and eyes
protuberant with grief, the staring
unbelief writhes bloodshot

in the tearless lids. The massed weirs
frozen of feeling are empty with disuse.
Without you without you without you
branches like nerves are sporadic with fever.

Yellow as dead flowers as a remembered South
yellow as desire as face to face
dawn with a handful of unnecessary hours
dawn with cut flowers and a mouth of disaster.

Alan Ross.

ARMISTICE

IN from the chintzy garden and the glare
he finds her in the cool cave of the room
straightening vases by the coloured hair,

patting the poll of a chrysanthemum
whose sentimental face nods back to her.

Collected. But the great gong of the heat
to which wild-rooted people blaze like a curtain,
is passion of liberty in male sun and root.
He nestles in the vase, and has forgotten
all but her firm caressings of his heart.

Unarm, Eros : fighting love is over ;
in from the battle, drinking through a stem
female charity for a flower or lover.
No more struggle, as hands or scissors come,
against possession or the power of the giver.

Abandoned now to love, but no more summer's
—enslaved for all the rest—we turn to look
at those who fought in love with hate like swimmers
in lava towards love to a white rock :
to Hero's vase.
                    Peace to the tents and rumours,
peace to the amorous air on sea and farm,
and lovers grown each other's superstition :
to all poor earth above the joy of the worm.
Only immortal longings are compassion :
a woman and a flower : Eros, unarm.

Terence Tiller.

INVOCATION
(*For Alec and Merula Guinness*)

I who was once a golden woman like those who walk
In the dark heavens—but am now grown old
And sit by the fire and see the fire grow cold
Watch the dark fields for a rebirth of faith and wonder.

The turning of Ixion's wheel the day
Ceased not, yet sounds no more the beat of the heart
But only the sound of ultimate Darkness falling
And of the blind Samson at the Fair, shaking the pillars of the world
                    and emptily calling.

For the gardeners cried for rain, but the high priests howled
For a darker rain to cool the delirium of gold
And wash the sore of the world, the heart of Dives,
Raise wheat for the hunger that lies in the soul of the poor . . .
Then came the thunderous the darkness,

And the fly-like whispering of small hopes, small fears—
The gossips of mean Death—gadflies and gnats, the summer world,
The small and gilded scholars of the Fly
That feed upon the crowds and their dead breath
And buzz and stink where the bright heroes die
Of the dust's rumours and the old world's fevers :
Then fell the world in winter.

But I, a golden woman like the corn-goddess
Watch the dark fields and know when spring begins
To the sound of the heart and the planetary rhythm,
Fires in the heavens and in the hearts of men,
Young people and young flowers come out in the darkness.

And where are they going ? How should I know ? I see only
The hierarchies love the young people—the Swan has given his
                    snows
And Berenice her wild mane to make their fair hair—
And speaking of love are the voices that come from the darkness—

Of the nobler love of Man to his brother Man
And of how the creeds of the world shall no more divide them,
But every life be that of a country Fate
Whose wheel has a golden woof and warp, the Day
—Woven of threads of the common task ; and light
Tells to that little child the humble dust

Tales of the old world's holiness, finds veins of ore
In the unripe wheat-ear ; and the common fire
That drops with seed like the Sun's, is fallen from the long-leaved
         planets.

So when the winter of the world and Man's fresh Fall
When democratic Death feared no more the heart's coldness
Shall be forgotten—
O love, return to the dying world, as the light
Of morning, shining in all regions, latitudes
And households of high heaven within the heart.

Be then our visible world, our world invisible!
Throughout our day like the laughing flames of the Sun
Lie on our leaves of life, your heat infusing
Deep in the amber blood of the smooth tree . . .
The panic splendour of the animal
Is yours—O primal Law
That rules the blood (the solar ray in the veins—
The fire of the hearth, the household Deity
That shines not, nor does it burn, destroy, like fire—
But nourishes with its endless wandering
Like that of the Golden Ones in the high heavens).

Rule then the spirit working in dark earth
As the sun and planets rule the husbandman—
O pride that in each semitone
Of amber blood and bone
Proclaims the splendour that arose from the first Dark !

Be too the ear of wheat to the Lost Men
Who ask the city stones if they are bread
And the stones of the city weep . . .
                        you, the lost days
When all might still be hoped for, and the light
Laid gold in the unhopeful path of the poor—
The shrunken darkness in the miser's heart.

Now falls the night of the world—O Spirit moving upon the waters
Your peace instil
In the animal heat and splendour of the blood,
The hot gold of the sun that flames in the night
And knows not down-going
But moves with the revolutions in the heavens.

The thunders and the fires and acclamations
Of the leaves of spring are stilled, but in the night
The Holy Ghost speaks in the whispering leaves . . .
O wheat-ear shining like a fire and the bright gold,
O water brought from far to the dying gardens!

Bring peace to the famine of the heart and lips,
And to the Last Man's loneliness
Of those who dream they can bring back sight to the blind.
You are the Night
When the long hunt for Nothing is at rest
In the Blind Man's Street, and in the human breast
The hammer of chaos is stilled.
                                Be then the sleep
When Judas gives again the childish kiss
That once his mother knew—and wash the stain
From the darkened hands of the universal Cain.

Edith Sitwell.

Notes.—' . . . the blood seeming . . . to have a share of another
diviner body, and being diffused with divine animal heat, suddenly
acquires remarkable and most excellent powers, and is analagous to
the essence of the stars. In so far as it is spirit, it is the hearth, the
Vesta, the household divinity, the innate heat, the sun of the
microcosm, the fire of Plato ; not because like common fire it
lightens, burns and destroys, but because by a vague and incessant
motion it preserves, nourishes and aggrandizes itself. It farther
deserves the name of spirit, inasmuch as it is radical moisture, at
once the ultimate and the proximate and the primary aliment . . .'—
The Works of William Harvey, M.D., translated by R. WILLIS.

'... through its (the blood's) tenuity and purity, says Aristotle
(De Part: Anim: lib. III), "animals are made wiser and have
more noble senses; and in like manner they are more timid and
courageous, or passionate and furious, as their blood is more dilate,
or replete with dense fibres." '—(Ibid: *On Generation.*)

THE ISLES OF GREECE

THE sun is not in love with us,
Nor the corrosive sea;
Yet both will burn our dried-up flesh
In deep intimacy

With stubborn tongues of briny death
And heavy snakes of fire,
Which writhe and hiss and crack the Greek
Myth of the singing lyre.

The dusty fig-tree cries for help,
Two peasants kill one snake,
While in our rocky heart the gods
Of marble hush and break.

After long ages all our love
Became a barren fever,
Which makes us glow in martyrdom
More beautiful than ever.

Yet when the burning horses force
Apollo to dismount
And rest with us at last, he says
That beauty does not count.

Demetrios Capetanakis.

[135]

LEANING IN THE EVENINGS

LEANING in the evenings, I live
    Between a dream and a tear;
The dogs of memory howling, shall
    Mourn on the steps of the heart.

Lost in the temporal labyrinth
    How shall I find that exit?
O follow backward the fallen face and the fragments
    Of desecrated existence!

Then everywhere I shall discover
    In a mnemonic room,
The spectre in a glass sepulchre
    With a child on its arm.

From the small tree calls to me
    The voice of the devoted
Turtle dove, that, forsaken in the myrtle,
    Utters the last of love.

' I wish you anguish and wild seas,
    Cataclysms and thunder,
So that in extremity you long for me
    And the bed of my gender.

The forked lightning, kicking
    Its gold legs across the sky,
Tells you how once, between my knees
    Fighting, you rose to die.'

The swan at midnight hangs its head
    Singing into my mirror;
And in the morning, by my bed,
    Lies still beside its fellow.

Then everywhere I discover
In a mnemonic room,
The spectre in a glass sepulchre
With a child on its arm.

George Barker.

THE SPHERE OF GLASS

So through the sun-laced woods they went
Where no one walked but two that day,
And they were poets, and content
Sharing the one deep-vistaed way,
Sister and brother to walk on
Where years like thickets round them lay.

It was the Roman dyke that ran
Between the bluebells and the fern,
The loam so fresh, they half began
To feel the bones deep under turn,
And, listening, dreamed their argument
Something from ancient death would learn.

One bird among the golden-green
Spangle of leaves was poised to sing :
They heard the opening trill, and then
Silence ; as if its heart could bring
No note so pure but would disturb
The soundless fountain of the Spring.

Within the wood, within that hour
It seemed a sphere of glass had grown
That glittered round their lives, with power
To link what grief the dyke had known
With voices of their vaster war
The sun-shot bombers' homing drone,

[137]

And make one tragic harmony
Where still this theme, their hope, returned,
And still the Spring unchangeably
In fires of its own sap was burned
And poetry, from love and death,
The peace their human contest earned.

It might have been all history
Without the sphere of wonder lay
And just beyond their colloquy
Some truth more pure than they could say,
While through the bluebells and the fern
Sister and brother made their way.

John Lehmann.

AT A TIME OF DEATH
(*In Memory of J.D.A., killed in Italy*)

WHO walks by the shore ?
A boy in the mist.
The white vapours twist
On the face of the sun,
And confound sea and land.
If they cleared, it might blind him
This day just begun,
As he walks by the shore
With his footprints in sand
So fleeting behind him
And his shadow before.

What cries by the shore ?
The seagulls that fly
Out of mist in the sky
Round the boy's puckered eyes,
And swoop to the sand

To the wrecks and the graves ;
He hears their weird cries
As he walks by the shore,
And far-off and at hand
Under all are the waves
With their pulse and their roar.

There are bones by the shore
In the pebbles and shells,
And the salt rotting smells
Of the things of the sea
Are mixed on the air
With a fragrance that comes
From each blossoming tree
Of gardens in-shore ;
Is it love waits him there ?
Is it nothingness drums
On the rocky sea-floor ?

Who walks by the shore ?
A boy who has seen
Where the mist had just been
Sudden end to the sands :
For the tall headland looms
Sheer in front, and the wave
Beats and boils where he stands.
And he walks from the shore
Where the sea-trumpet booms
In whorls of its cave,
And is known here no more.

John Lehmann.

THE REVENANT

Out of the famous canyon
Deeper than sleep,
From the nerveless tarn of oblivion

She climbed. Dark was the slope,
And her companion
Gave not one love-glance back to brighten it.
Only a wind-chafed rope
Of melody held her
To him that haled her
Lifeward, praising the fire and delight in it.

On the gist of that lay or its burden
Legend is dumb.
How else, though, with love-looks forbidden,
Could he say, ' Come back to me, come '—
Could he touch the long-hidden
Spring of a shade unfleshed, unfertilised
Than by singing, oh, crust and crumb,
Bark, sap, flesh, marrow—
Life's all, in the narrow
Ambit of sense flowering immortalised ?

Glimmering tall through the gloom
In her phantom garment,
Like a daffodil when its stem
Feels trembling the first endearment
Of amorous bloom,
She palely paused, on the verge of light again,
One step to break from her cerement—
Yes, daffodil-rayed
From the mould of the shade—
No revenant now, a golden wife again.

Had death become then, already,
A habit too strong
For her to break ? The steady
Pulsing of Orpheus' song
—Though lightwards led he—
Grew faint in her heart. She wept for astonishment,
Feared she could never belong

To life, be at home there,
Find aught but harm there,
Till that last step seemed less a birth than a banishment.

What strand of his love was the weak one—
Nay, how it befell
That a song which could melt the Dark One,
Death's granite lord, with its spell
Saved not his meek one,
Moved not his meek one to step from the last of her
Terrors—no man may tell.
He felt the cord parting,
The death wound smarting:
He turned his head but to glimpse the ghost of her.

So, as a pebble thrown
From a cliff face, soaring
Swerves back, less like a stone
Than a bird, ere it falls to the snoring
Surf, she was gone.
Reluctant her going: but the more bitterly
Mocked were his love, his imploring—
That the gods spoke
As seldom they speak
On matters of life and death, non-committally.

C. Day Lewis.

THE DIVIDED WAYS
(*In Memory of Sidney Keyes*)

HE has gone down into the dark cellar
To talk with the bright-faced Spirit with silver hair;
But I shall never know what word was spoken there.

.   .   .   .   .

My friend is out of earshot; our ways divided
Before we even knew we had missed each other.

For he advanced
Into a stony wilderness of the heart,
Under a hostile and red-clawed Sun ;
All that dry day, until the darkness fell,
I heard him going, and shouting among the canyons.
But I, struck backward from the Eastern Gate,
Had turned aside, obscure,
Beneath the unfriendly silence of the Moon,
My long white fingers on a small carved lute.
There was a forest, and faces known in childhood
Rose unexpected from the mirrored pools ;
The trees had hands to clutch my velvet shoulders,
And birds of fever sang among the branches ;
Till the dark vine-boughs, breaking as I seized them,
And dripping blood, cried out with my own voice :
' I also have known thirst, and the wanderer's terror! . . .'

But I had lost my friend and the mountain paths.
And if there might have been another meeting—
The new Sun rising in a different sky,
Having repaired his light in the streams of Ocean,
And the Moon, white and maternal, going down
Over the virgin hills—it is too late
Ever to find it now.

And though it was in May that the reptile guns
And breeze-fly bullets took my friend away,
It is not time to forge a delicate idyll
Of the young shepherd, stricken, prone among
The flowers of Spring, heavy with morning dew,
And emblematic blood of dying gods :
Or that head pillowed on a wave's white fleece,
Softly drowning in a Celtic sea.
This was more harsh and meaningless than Winter.

But now, at last, I dare avow my terror
Of the pale vampire by the cooling grate ;
The enemy face that doubled every loved one ;

My secret fear of him and his cold heroes ;
The meaning of the dream
Which was so fraught with trouble for us both;
And how, through this long autumn
(Sick and tempestuous with another sorrow)
His spirit, vexed, fluttered among my thoughts,
A bird returning to the darkened window—
The hard-eyed albatross with scissor bill.
And I would ask his pardon for this weakness.

But he is gone where no hallooing voice
Or beckoning hand may ever call him back ;
And what is ours of him
Must speak impartially for all the world.
There is no personal word remains for me,
And I pretend to find no meaning here.
Though I might guess that other Singer's wisdom
Who saw in Death a dark immaculate flower
And tenderness in every falling Autumn,
This abstract music will not bring again
My friend to his warm room.
Inscrutable the darkness covers him.

John Heath-Stubbs.

LANDSCAPE NEAR TOBRUK

THIS land was made for War. As glass
Resists the bite of vitriol, so this hard
And calcined earth rejects
The battle's hot, corrosive impact. Here
Is no nubile, girlish land, no green
And virginal countryside for War
To violate. This land is hard,

[143]

Inviolable ; the battle's aftermath
Presents no ravaged and emotive scene,
No landscape à la Goya. Here are no trees
Uprooted, gutted farms ; the unsalvaged scrap—
The scattered petrol-cans, the upturned
And abandoned truck, the fallen Heinkel : all
The rusted and angular detritus
Of war, seem scarcely to impinge
Upon the harsh resistant surface of
This lunar land : ephemeral
As trippers' leavings, paper-bags and orange-peel
Upon Ben Nevis. Sun and sand
Inhibit here the mind's habitual
And easy gestures ; hand and eye
Perform their functions with a robot-cunning—
The sly and casual movements of
The shadowed thief. The soldiers camped
In the rock-strewn wadi merge
Like lizard or jerboa in the brown
And neutral ambient : stripped at gunsite,
Or splashing like glad beasts at sundown in
The brackish pool, their smooth
And lion-coloured bodies seem
The indigenous fauna of an unexplored,
Unspoiled country : harmless, easy to trap,
And tender-fleshed—a hunter's prize.

Jocelyn Brooke.

WAR POET

WE in our haste can only see the small components of the scene
We cannot tell what incidents will focus on the final screen.
A barrage of disruptive sound, a petal on a sleeping face,
Both must be noted, both must have their place ;

It may be that our later selves or else our unborn sons
Will search for meaning in the dust of long deserted guns,
We only watch, and indicate and make our scribbled pencil notes.
We do not wish to moralize, only to ease our dusty throats.

Donald Bain.

ICARUS
(for Noel)

I WRITE not knowing whether
Icarus lives or is dead
If the sun has melted the wax the wax
Or the gunfire Brueghel's earth :
Death Death Death
In the Mediterranean basin
And his crest was a light blue wingy horse
On a mulberry mulberry flag.

On the Oxford Bypass
In a powerful car
Crisp, crisp in command of men,
With my braided blouse
And sharp peaked cap,
And weaving up the road to Wales
The proud young despatch riders jockey the column
Going to practice killing laughing.

Who left his younger brother
In the deep-gabled house
And the garden Tennysonian
All moonlight grace.

O who will come on a trip to Jerusalem
From the pub still called The Trip to Jerusalem
In English Nottingham ?
No, not for justice, right, or democracy,
But to follow the crusaders their king ?

Beyond the file of poplars the still lake
Waits in silence for the whispering canoe
That Hugh built with Michael ; you recollect
Involuntarily one whispers, out at night,
And paddled round the islets all night long
Until the morning came in a white mist.

' It is curious, ' the commentator said
At the departure of the Crusade,
' That I see no king only
An empty suit of armour on a horse,
The visor open and no face.'

O Icarus, the air is thin
And you may not walk on light,
Surely you should have known
Why you would tempt the sun,
Why this blue-pinioned horse
And fealty to the outline king.

                                   W. F. M. Stewart.

THE JUNGLE

I

IN mole-blue indolence the sun
Plays idly on the stagnant pool
In whose grey bed black swollen leaf
Holds Autumn rotting like an unfrocked priest.
The crocodile slides from the ochre sand
And drives the great translucent fish
Under the boughs across the running gravel.
Windfalls of brittle mast crunch as we come
To quench more than our thirst—our selves—
Beneath this bamboo bridge, this mantled pool
Where sleep exudes a sinister content
As though all strength of mind and limb must pass

And all fidelities and doubts dissolve,
The weighted world a bubble in each head,
The warm pacts of the flesh betrayed
By the nonchalance of a laugh,
The green indifference of this sleep.

II

Wandering and fortuitous the paths
We followed to this rendezvous to-day
Out of the mines and offices and dives,
The sidestreets of anxiety and want,
Huge cities known and distant as the stars,
Wheeling beyond our destiny and hope.
We did not notice how the accent changed
As shadows ride from precipice and plain
Closing the parks and cordoning the roads,
Clouding the humming cultures of the West—
The weekly bribe we paid the man in black,
The day shift sinking from the sun,
The blinding arc of rivets blown through steel,
The patient queues, headlines and slogans flung
Across a frightened continent, the town
Sullen and out of work, the little home
Semi-detached, suburban, transient
As fever or the anger of the old,
The best ones on some specious pretext gone.
But we who dream beside this jungle pool
Prefer the instinctive rightness of the poised
Pied kingfisher deep darting for a fish
To all the banal rectitude of states,
The dew-bright diamonds on a viper's back
To the slow poison of a meaning lost
And the vituperations of the just.

III

The banyan's branching clerestories close
The noon's harsh splendour to a head of light.

The black spot in the focus grows and grows :
The vagueness of the child, the lover's deep
And inarticulate bewilderment,
The willingness to please that made a wound,
The kneeling darkness and the hungry prayer ;
Cargoes of anguish in the holds of joy,
The smooth deceitful stranger in the heart,
The tangled wrack of motives drifting down
An oceanic tide of wrong.
And though the state has enemies we know
The greater enemy within ourselves.

Some things we cleaned like knives in earth,
Kept from the dew and rust of Time
Instinctive truths and elemental love,
Knowing the force that brings the teal and quail
From Turkestan across the Himalayan snows
To Kashmir and the South alone can guide
That winging wilderness home again.

Oh you who want us for ourselves,
Whose love can start the snow-rush in the woods
And melt the glacier in the dark coulisse,
Forgive this strange inconstancy of soul,
The face distorted in a jungle pool
That drowns its image in a mort of leaves.

IV

Grey monkeys gibber, ignorant and wise.
We are the ghosts, and they the denizens ;
We are like them anonymous, unknown,
Avoiding what is human, near,
Skirting the villages, the paddy fields
Where boys sit timelessly to scare the crows
On bamboo platforms raised above their lives.
A trackless wilderness divides
Joy from its cause, the motive from the act :

The killing arm uncurls, strokes the soft moss ;
The distant world is an obituary,
We do not hear the tappings of its dread.
The act sustains ; there is no consequence.
Only aloneness, swinging slowly
Down the cold orbit of an older world
Than any they predicted in the schools,
Stirs the cold forest with a starry wind,
And sudden as the flashing of a sword
The dream exalts the bowed and golden head
And time is swept with a great turbulence,
The old temptation to remould the world.

The bamboos creak like an uneasy house ;
The night is shrill with crickets, cold with space.
And if the mute pads on the sand should lift
Annihilating paws and strike us down
Then would some unimportant death resound
With the imprisoned music of the soul ?
And we become the world we could not change ?

Or does the will's long struggle end
With the last kindness of a foe or friend ?

Alun Lewis.

LAZARUS

THIS knock means death. I heard it once before
As I was struggling to remember one,
Just one thing, crying in my fever for
Help, help. Then the door opened, yet no Son

Came in to whisper what I had to know.
Only my sisters wetted me with tears,
But tears are barren symbols. Love is slow,
And when she comes she neither speaks nor hears :

[149]

She only kisses and revives the dead
Perhaps in vain. Because what is the use
Of miracles unheard-of, since instead
Of trying to remember the great News

Revealed to me alone by Death and Love,
I struggled to forget them and become
Like everybody else ? I longed to move
As if I never had been overcome

By mysteries which made my sisters shiver
As they prepared the supper for our Friend.
He came and we received Him as the Giver,
But did not ask Him when our joy would end.

And now I hear the knock I heard before,
And strive to make up for the holy time,
But I cannot remember, and the door
Creaks letting in my unambiguous crime.

Demetrios Capetanakis.

TO HIMSELF

Now be for ever still,
Weary my heart. For the last cheat is dead,
I thought eternal. Dead. For us, I know
Not only the dear hope
Of being deluded gone, but the desire.
Rest still for ever. You
Have beaten long enough. And to no purpose
Were all your stirrings ; earth not worth your sighs.
For spleen and bitterness
Is life ; and the rest, nothing ; the world is dirt.
Lie quiet now. Despair

For the last time. Fate granted to our kind
Only the dying. Now you may despise
Yourself, nature, the brute
Power which hidden, ordains the common doom,
And all the immeasurable emptiness of things.

John Heath-Stubbs.
(from the Italian of Leopardi.)

THE EVENING AFTER THE HOLY DAY

THE night is soft and clear, and no wind blows ;
The quiet moon stands over roofs and orchards
Revealing from afar each peaceful hill.
Sweetheart, now every field-path is silent ;
At intervals along the balconies
The night-long lantern gleams : you are asleep,
And gentle slumber now gathers about
Your quiet chamber, and no single care
Gnaws at your heart ; you do not know at all,
Nor think that you have opened in my breast
A very grievous wound. You are asleep :
And I have come abroad to reverence
This sky whose aspect seems to be so gentle,
And ancient Nature powerful over all,
Who has fashioned me for trouble. ' I deny
All hope to you,' she has said, ' Yea, even hope ;
Your eyes shall not be bright for any cause,
Except with weeping.' This was a festal day :
And you are resting after its amusements ;
And maybe in your dreams you still remember
How many eyes took pleasure in your beauty,
How many, too, pleased you : I find no place—
Not that I hoped it now—among your thoughts.

Meantime I ask how many years of life
Remain to me ; and then it is I cast
Myself upon the ground, and cry, and rage.
Oh terrible days, even of our green youth!
Alas, I hear not far along the road
The lonely singing of a workman, coming
Back to his poor home so late at night,
After the sports ; and fiercely my heart aches
Thinking how all this world passes away
And leaves no trace. For look, the festival
Is over now ; an ordinary day
Succeeds to-morrow ; all things our race has known
Time likewise bears away. Where now is the voice
Of the ancient peoples, the clamour of our ancestors
Who were renowned, and that great Empire of Rome,
The arms, and the clash they made by land and sea ?
All is silence and peace ; the world is still ;
There are no tidings now remain of them.
Once in my boyhood, when so eagerly
We would look forward to the holiday,
Finding it over, I lay upon my bed,
Wakeful and very unhappy ; late that night
A singing heard along the field-paths,
Little by little dying into the distance,
Even as this does now, pierced through my heart.

John Heath-Stubbs.
(from the Italian of Leopardi.)

THE HANGING CHURCH

BASKING in typical decrepitude,
The Romans' and Josephus' Babylon,
Old Cairo, prone, exposes to the sun

Its faceless slums, its multitude
Of shrieking hawking creatures. While
The noonday heat begins to strike
We through that ancient squalor file
To where the fortress lifts its dyke
Out of the dusty rising plain
Between Mokattam and the Nile :
And, scattering in the usual filthy lane
The usual goats and children, reach the porch
Below the entrance to the Hanging Church.

Curiously straitened, it survives to please.
Clinging to the old fortress like a nest
Built out of mud by some bird's beak and breast,
For centuries on centuries
It has been threatened, yet we see
The painted saints, the screens and doors
That shut upon the sanctuary.
Their cedar-wood inlaid with scores
Of little crosses, they express
A dense and dazzling geometry
Appropriate to a narrowed saintliness,
And are doctrinal in their intricacy
Of inlaid ebony and ivory.

And was it here the Holy Family
Sheltered when their new wonder was oppressed
And threatened narrowly ? The place at least
Fits the myth well. The crypt is shown where (we
Are told) they lived three months. The Virgin's eyes
In this dim picture that we see
Large, open, oval, almond-wise
Drawn in black pencil lucidly—
Follow us round, a thing we're shown
As some unheard-of rarity.
—Yes, but she held and holds what is her own
As we do not. Her gaze as we go on
Follows, in that devout phenomenon.

[153]

Cruel pressures made this place, like those we doubt.
Must all our love take refuge, crouch and perch
Between two bastions like the Hanging Church
Niched in its fortress ? Coming out
I wonder whether I shall be
Like some stern figure on a door
Of ebony or ivory,
Demetrius or Theodore—
Taciturn, staring, tutelary,
A great-eyed wooden effigy
Riding a wooden horse : his adversary
Lies stiffly in the dust while on his right
Sits, lonely as himself, a guardian kite.

F. T. Prince.

ALMOND BLOSSOM IN WARTIME

FLOWERING almond tree,
Angelically you bring
With praying hands, bent knee
And arc of coral-petalled wing,
Annunciation of spring.

Your message burning like a taper
Unfolds translucent petals, here
Where jagged column broken stair
—Silhouettes of torn paper—
Upbraid the azure dome of air.

O lift us to those skies
—Which, through interstices
Of your leaves and petals show
Their cold and scattered eyes—

[154]

To the wild sun above the snow,
Moulder of southern masterpieces,
Whose whirling fires create
Dazzling petals from dark fate.

Stephen Spender.

EL AGHIR

SPRAWLED on the bags and crates in the rear of the truck,
I was gummy-mouthed from the sun and the dust of the track ;
And the two Arab soldiers I'd taken on as hitch-hikers,
At a torrid petrol-dump, had been there on their hunkers
Since early morning. I said, in a kind of French,
' On m'a dit qu'il y a une belle source d'eau fraîche,
Plus loin, à El Aghir.' It was eighty more kilometres
Until round a corner we heard a splashing of waters,
And there, in a green, dark street, was a fountain with two facers,
Discharging both ways, from full-throated faucets
Into basins, then into troughs and then into brooks.
Our negro corporal driver slammed his brakes,
And we yelped and leapt from the truck and went at the double
To fill our bidons and bottles and drink and dabble.
Then, swollen with water, we went to an inn for wine.
The Arabs came, too, though their creed might have stood between;
' After all,' they said, ' it's a boisson ', without contrition.

Green, green is El Aghir. It has a railway station,
And the wealth of its soil has borne many another fruit,
A mairie, a school and an elegant Salle de Fêtes.
Such blessings, as I remarked, in effect, to the waiter,
Are added unto them that have plenty of water.

Norman Cameron.

UNSEEN FIRE

THIS is a damned unnatural sort of war;
The pilot sits above the clouds, quite sure
About the values he is fighting for;
He cannot hear beyond his vale of sound,

He cannot see the people on the ground;
He only knows that on the sloping map
Of sea-fringed town and country people creep
Like ants—and who cares if ants laugh or weep?

To us he is no more than a machine
Shown on an instrument; what can he mean
In human terms—a man, somebody's son,
Proud of his skill; compact of flesh and bone
Fragile as Icarus—and our desire
To see that damned machine come down on fire?

R. N. Currey.

CASUALTY

DEATH stretched down two hands,
One on desert sands
Shut his eyes. The other in her head
Opened the third eye of ruin; instead
Of doubt, which veiled it, certainty now gives it sight,
Staring dark and twitching when she sleeps at night,
When she wakes turning her, indifferent, from light.

Sometimes looking through a door into a sunny room, cold,
Full of furniture, but empty except for herself, old
In the mirror. Sometimes resting on fields flowing their green gold
Flowers, giving her an illusion of summer, but her thawing tear

Freezes quickly in the eternal ice of confirmed fear.
Sometimes, drifting along the canal of fatigue, he seems near,
The eye is closing—then suddenly starts in her brain,
Opens—He is gone. She, with walls, iron-coloured rain,
Railings silhouetted either side, is alone again.

We, who for our own comfort, imagined that a grief,
Could be smoothed and stroked by time to its relief,
Looking at her face, know now that only their brief
Past stands. The sun has equal entrance there
With mist or wind. We move in talking where
Gates stood—but voices fade,
Transfixed, in her stone shade.

Diana Witherby.

THE BREEZES OF FREEDOM

The breezes of freedom blow all round me!
My body, like the standing harp left
Idle in the midst of the moaning orchestra,
Trembles quietly,
Forgotten by the pains, by suffering,
Forgotten by necessity.
I listen to the quiet resound :
Resonator of the universe,
Secret, imperceptible response,
—O miracle of love!—
Top of a high tree
Moved by the songs of the birds.

Pantelis Prevelakis.
(*Translated from the Greek by* D. CAPETANAKIS.)

THE WORD OF DEATH
(*For Demetrios Capetanakis*)

FAR from the crux, the thinking dome,
     Or carnal love's
Soft pull of muscle in the night,
Exists the pure mobility
Of endless concentration without Name.

There words in useless glitter fall,
     And only one,
Shaped by the greed of many men,
Moves like a sable butterfly,
And wears the certain vehemence of Fate.

Let it descend, rest in all thought;
     Hear once again
Death offer Oneness like a bribe,
And haunt the windows of the world
With living's Prisoner imagined free.

Peter Yates.

LAMENT FOR THE SLEEPWALKER

THE lion is like him and the elusive leopard:
Nine lived, he ranges—killer cat—my heart.
Green is the hanging moss, and green the jungle
Creeper: green where the gold plantations part
Their bamboo branches for a murderer's head.
In green courts he eats meat from the green dead.

See, like a rajah, how he ravens fine food.
The long claws fork their lightning; diamond, his teeth,
Glitter of jewel jaws, dazzle—glaze their mirrors

[158]

Black blood and purple, stained points of glass. Beneath
Lascivious fur, his regal muscles flex,
Digesting fire, the marrow root of sex.

At bat-call sleeps : at serpent hour is waking,
My beautiful and butcher beast, once more
The prowler from the palms ; and stalks, O hunter
Hidden in death's ambuscade, love going before
The daylight with a levelled spear. What time
He gives by lemon tree, he takes by lime.

Sprung from his high point, Tiglon, Prince of Asia,
His forepaw threads through scarlet sockets—blind
Since the great nails pitted sapphire : ice-tipped needles,
Magnetic to their lodestar, flashing, find
Out violet veins, whose midnight rivers race
To Golconda for their trysting place.

Where skullbone banners, no pity flags, are flying
Before the cruel and radium caves, he lairs
His treasure. There, while jackals scream, Lord Vulture,
Wing caged in crystal, sings his subtle airs
Of praise ; recalls how orchid adder hissed
Above the crypt when lion and lover kissed.

Nightmare is livelong by a never-ending :
In the most mandrake forest, I walk, love lost,
Through panther grass towards no good morrow. Agave
Leaves like hundred years impale my ghost
On yesterdays of youth. At crossroad stands
The stranger with his four and frantic hands.

Dunstan Thompson.
(U.S.A.)

SUMMER RAIN

WHERE in the valley the summer rain
Moves crazed and chill through the crooked trees
The briars bleed green, and the far fox-banks
Their sharp cries tangle in sobbing shades.

I hear the sad rinsing of reeded meadows
The small lakes rise in the wild white rose
The shudder of wings in the streaming cedars
And tears of lime running down from the hills.

All day in the tomb of my brain I hear
The cold wheat whisper, the veiled trees mourn,
And behold through windows of weighted ivy
The wet walls blossom with silver snails.

The heron flies up from the stinging waters,
The white swan droops by the dripping reed,
The summer lies swathed in its ripeness, exuding
Damp odours of lilies and alabaster.

In a fever of June she is wrapped and anointed
With deathly sweating of cold jasmine,
And her petals weep wax to the thick green sky
Like churchyard wreaths under domes of glass.

Too long hangs the light in the valley lamenting,
The slow rain sucking the sun's green eye;
And too long do you hide in your vault of clay
While I search for your passion's obliterated stone.

Let the dark night come, let its crack of doom
The sky's heart shatter and empty of grief,
The storm fetch its thunder of hammers and axes,
The green hills break as our graves embrace.

Laurie Lee.

ELEGY

I

A PICTURE buried
In a black steel box
Down in the country
Out of harm's way
Assists no memory by the sandy shore
Nor where the wind cavorts among the mountains
Nor in a quiet room, where voices,
Some trick of movement, one
Held for a moment, out of many faces,
Recall a face now hidden from the sun,
That looked at something, and observing changed it;
And a voice that played with,
Tossed and toppled
Over the shoulder and out through the window
And over the roofs towards
The sea and the outbound ships
Chains of links of clanging words
Clinging and clotted, coupled and uncoupled
Clattering away from your lips.

II

Over the flat shore the birds
Leaning on easy wings, are level with the hills.
The light of evening spills
Over the sand and the pools under the rocks
Reflecting the far-flown gulls that over the sea have ferried
An image connecting and resurrecting
Something that I have buried
(That the dead may come to no harm)
In a black steel box
Down on a country farm.

III

When the memory is warm
We watch it settle and cool

And when we do not watch it
It cools behind our backs.
Does it, when it is older
Grow cold till it is colder
Than even the salty pool
That lies under the rocks ?
Or may it, having once struck out a spark
Warming as well as lighting up the dark
Combine with others so to heat the room
That even the accidental knife
That cuts away a bleeding part
From the matrix of our heart
That rounds our ultimate synthesis like a womb,
May make a wound the pain of which
Even if only a recurrent itch
Can last as long as life ?
If we were certain so to be dismembered,
Our feet cut off at ankles, hands at wrists,
Till what is left is stripped of skin
And exquisitely sensitized all over,
Each facet sure to be remembered—
Such evidence that all exists
Compelling us to draw our tendrils in—
Which one of us would ever take a lover ?

IV

Perhaps because we kill
What of the past in us
Does not seem deserved,
Some counterpoising will
Restores the balance thus.

Perhaps the surfeit checks
By its own mechanism
What we do not merit—
But O what ships it wrecks
In every cataclysm.

All of the trees that now
Overhang us here
Turn their faces to us ;
So for the sheep and cow
The sky's a hemisphere.

V

The astronomers of the Chaldees sat up late ;
Each of them sat and plotted out a graph,
Seeking and finding in the chart of half
The stars the world can see
The macrocosmography
Of theirs and of their masters' fate.
They plotted against the truth erecting
Umbrella-spokes inside the dome, connecting
All that they saw with one fixed point ;
Where they made the axial joint
They built themselves a focal place for forces,
And standing there, ring-mastered all the courses
Of all the planets making them circus horses,
And cracked their whips
At the distant stars
To guide their ships
And win their wars.

VI

But for us the gulls, flying over the seas
Out in the bay, riding the western breeze
If we could follow them, cross at last the line
Where mine becomes yours, and where yours is mine.
And eyes that strain
After their flight
Seek to suffer the pain
In the horizon's light.
When at the rising sun
Waves refract its glow
Cold in the slant of dawn,

The white-winged carriers go
Carrying back the answer
To the land that holds the grave,
Words that flit like dancer
Over every wave :
' Not a land beyond the seas
But a land under our feet,
Our fates' Antipodes
Is where we two shall meet.
In a chest your face is buried
And in a box your heart
But above your forehead
The sky is a different chart.
What it is now was always
Common to you and me,
Something we guessed in hallways
Or sitting and drinking tea,
Moments we apprehended,
Hard shapes behind the mist
That became, when we tried to bend them
Stronger than our wrists ;
Some pattern that lies under
The patterns we observe,
Some counterpointing, tender
Completion of the curve
Round which I must pursue
The course I hold unshaken
To meet the straight way through,
Since we have undertaken
That I, when I shall grow old,
And you that keep your youth,
Shall neither of us yield
And plot against the truth.'

Maurice James Craig.

OFLAG NIGHT PIECE

THERE, where the swifts flicker along the wall
And the last light catches—there in the high schloss
(How the town grows dark) all's made impregnable :
They bless each window with a double cross
Of iron ; weave close banks of wire and train
Machine guns down them ; and look—at the first star
Floodlight the startled darkness back again . . .
All for three hundred prisoners of war.
Yet now past them and the watch they keep,
Unheard, invisible, in ones and pairs,
In groups, in companies—alarms are dumb,
A sentry loiters, a blind searchlight stares—
Unchallenged as their memories of home
The vanishing prisoners escape to sleep.

Michael Riviere.

ST. LUKE'S SUMMER

THE low sun leans across the slanting field,
And every blade of grass is striped with shine
And casts its shadow on the blade behind,
And dandelion clocks are held
Like small balloons of light above the ground.

Beside the trellis of the bowling-green
The poppy shakes its pepper-box of seed ;
Groundsel feathers flutter down ;
Roses exhausted by the thrust of summer
Lose grip and fall ; the wire is twined with weed.

The soul, too, has its brown October days—
The fancy run to seed and dry as stone,

[165]

Rags and whisps of words blown through the mind ;
And yet while dead leaves clog the eyes
Never-predicted poetry is sown.

Norman Nicholson.

IN PACHINO NOW

In Pachino now, where I shall be to-morrow,
Men at this moment are being wounded and dying :
Bullets are turning through a third dimension,
While I watch the flat drama of the screen, more real
Than the fear of death which stultifies the sense.

Or I watch the strangest element, the sea,
As the parched coast of Africa recedes,
Like a patient lulled after night's fever
Dreading the lights out and dark's falling
Yet lured by delirium with its vivid dreams.

At lunch across the cutlery and linen,
Over the polished glasses and our silence,
We hear the news that the landings have succeeded,
Beaches secured by 0600 ; beaches where we shall land
When the tables are silent again and empty to-morrow.

Or I sit on deck and the sunlight soothes me
Into a summer's memory ; and across the sea
Porpoises flicker in suburb gardens.
Sea, land, home and this distance mingle
To strike no image deeper than my useless longing.

There is nothing to analyse but the film of fear
Unwinding pictures of loved places in the eye,
The quiet drama that whispers, under the shelling,
Of a wife and wonder breaking in the stars :
Pity is choked under the dark of waiting.

H. B. Mallalieu.

A SONG OF THE COLD
(*To Natasha Litvin*)

HUGE is the sun of amethysts and rubies
And in the purple perfumes of the polar sun
And homeless cold they wander.
But winter is the time for comfort, and for friendship,
For warmth and food,
And a talk beside a fire like the Midnight Sun
—A glowing heart of amber and of musk. Time to forget
The falling night of the world and heart, the polar chaos
That separates us each from each. It is no time to roam
Along the pavements wide and cold as Hell's huge polar street,
Drifting along the city like the wind
Blowing aimlessly, and with no home
To rest in, only famine for a heart—
While Time means nothing to one, as to the wind
Who only cares for ending and beginning.

Here in the fashionable quarters of the city
Cold as the universal blackness of Hell's day
The two opposing brotherhoods are swept
Down the black marble pavements, Lethe's river.
First come the worlds of Misery, the small and tall Rag-Castles,
Shut off from every other . . . These have no name,
Nor friend to utter it . . . these of the extinct faces
Are a lost civilization, and have no possession
But the night and day, those centuries of cold.
Even their tears are changed now to the old
Eternal nights of ice round the loveless head
Of those who are lone and sexless as the Dead.
Dives of the Paleocrystic heart, behold
These who were once your brothers! Hear their voices
Hoarsened by want to the rusty voice of the Tiger, no more crying
The death of the soul, but lamenting their destitution.
What life, what solar system of the heart
Could bring a restitution
To these who die of the cold?

Some keep their youthful graces
Yet in their winding-sheets of rags seem early
Made ready for the grave . . . Worn to the bone by their famine
As if by the lusts that the poor Dead have known—
Who now are cold for ever . . . Those who are old
Seem humbler, lean their mouths to the earth as if to crop
The kind earth's growth—for this is the Cainozoic period
When we must learn to walk with the gait of the Ape and Tiger :
The warmth of the heart is dead, or has changed to the world's fever,
And love is but masked murder, the lust for possession,
The hunger of the Ape, or the confession
Of the last fear, the wish to multiply
Their image, of a race on oblivion's brink.

Lazarus, weep for those who have known the lesser deaths.
                              O think
How we should pity the High Priests of the god of this
                    world, the saints of Mammon,
The cult of gold! For see how these too ache with the cold
From the polar wastes of the heart . . . See all they have given
Their God! Are not their veins grown ivy-old
And have they not eaten their own hearts and lives in their famine ?

Their huge Arithmetic is but the endless
Repetition of Zero—the unlimited
Eternal. Even the beat of the heart and pulse is changed to this :
The counting of small deaths, the repetition
Of Nothing, endless positing and suppression of Nothing.
                    . . . So they live
And die of inanition . . .
                    The miser Foscue
Weaving his own death and sinking like a spider
To vaults and depths that held his gold, that Sun,
Was walled in that grave by the rotting hand of the dust,
                    by a trapdoor falling.
Do the enormous rays of the Sun now warm his blood,
                    the appalling
Empty gulf of his veins, or fertilize

His flesh, that continent of dryness ? . . . Yellow, cold,
And crumbling as his gold,
Deserted by the god of this world, a Gold Man like a terrible Sun,
A Mummy with a Lion's mane
He sits in this desert where no sound of wave shall come,
And Time's sands are of gold, filling his ears and eyes ;
And he who has grown the talons of the Lion
Has devoured the flesh of his own hands and heart in his pain.

Pity these hopeless acolytes . . . the vain
Prudence that emulates the wisdom of the Spider
Who spins but for herself—a world of Hunger
Constructed for the needs of Hunger! . . . Soon
Their blankets will be thinner than her thread :
When comes the night when they had only gold
For flesh, for warmth, for sheet—
O who would not pity these,
Grown fleshless, too, as those who starve and freeze!

Now falls the Night on Lazarus and Dives—
Those who were brothers, those who shared the pain
Of birth and lusts, and the lesser daily deaths,
The beat of the dying heart, the careful breaths :
' You are so worn to the bone, I thought you were Death,
                    my brother,
Death who will warm my heart ' . . . ' Have you, too,
                    known the cold ?
Give me your hand to warm me : I am no more alone!
There was a sun that shone
On all alike, but the cold in the heart of Man
Has slain it. Where is it gone ? '
So in the great Night that comes like love, they lie
As small as when they lay close to their mother's breast,
Naked and bare in their mortality.

Soon comes the Night when those who have never loved
Shall know the small immortal serpent's kiss
And turn to dust as lover turns to lover . . .
Then all shall know the cold's equality.

Young Beauty, bright as the tips of the budding vine,
You with the gold Appearances from Nothing rise
In the spring wind and but for a moment shine !

Dust are the temples that were bright as heat . . .
And, perfumed nosegay brought for noseless Death,
Your brightest myrrh can not perfume his breath ! . . .

That old rag-picker blown along the street
Was once great Venus. But now Age unkind
Has shrunken her so feeble and so small,
Weak as a babe. And she who gave the Lion's kiss
Has now all Time's gap for her piteous mouth.
What lullaby will Death sing, seeing this
Small babe ? And she of the golden feet
To what love does she haste ? After these centuries
The sun's will be her only kiss—now she is blackened,
                    shrunken, old
As the small worm—her kiss, like his, grown cold.

In the nights of spring, the inner leaf of the heart
Feels warm, and we will pray for the eternal cold
Of those who are only warmed by the sins of the world,
And those whose nights were violent like the buds
And roots of spring, but like the spring, grew old.
Their hearts are tombs on the heroic shore
That were of iris, diamond, hyacinth,
And now are patterned only by Time's wave . . . the glittering plinth
Is crumbling . . . But the great sins and fires break out of me
Like the terrible leaves from the bough in the violent spring . . .
I am a walking fire, I am all leaves—
I will cry to the Spring to give me the birds' and the serpents' speech
That I may weep for those who die of the cold—
The ultimate cold within the heart of Man.

Edith Sitwell.

Notes.—Verse 1, line 2.   ' There was the morning when, with
Her, you struggled amongst those banks of snow, those green-

lipped crevasses, that ice, those black flags and blue rays, and the purple perfumes of the polar sun.' Arthur Rimbaud, *Metropolitan*, translated by Helen Rootham.

Verse 1, line 4. 'Winter is the time for friendship.' This was occasioned in my mind by a phrase from *Une Saison en Enfer*.

Verse 1, line 7. 'This evening, Devotion to Circeto of the tall mirrors, fat as a fish and glowing like the ten mouths of the red night (her heart is of amber and musk).' Arthur Rimbaud. *Devotion*.

Verse 4. 'Zero must be endlessly positing itself, for in every respect it is indefinite or unlimited, eternal . . . The whole of Arithmetic is nothing but the endless repetition of Nothing, endless positing and suppression of Nothing.' Lorenz Oken. *Elements of Physiophilosophy*.

Verse 4, line 7. 'The miser of Foscue.' A farmer-general of France, existing in Languedoc about 1762. This verse tells the actual history of his fate.

Verse 7, line 6. 'The appearances which spring up of themselves in sleep or by day.' Plato. *Sophist*.

THE NEUROTICS

WE are the double people, gaoled and gaoler,
Sparrow and hawk in one uneasy body;
We are a battlefield but cannot clearly
Remember why the fight or when it started.

We are the builders of small doorless houses,
Walls to defy the other world which always
Peers in at us through widening cracks that vainly
We cram with mud or paper or our fingers.

Some of us build our secret world by gathering
Fans or old playing cards or Balkan watches
To hoard and pattern, love and list and label :
Kingdom in which we're king and none may enter.

Some of us build our world with pornographic
Postcards or drugs or mistresses or money,
Private religions or a cipher diary
Or great inventions in an attic drawer.

Some of us spend our lives preventing others
From doing what cannot or we dare not,
And stand in shadow spitting at the sunlight,
And watch at keyholes for the Day of Judgment.

Some of us play at games with blood and nightmares,
Pricking a tender nerve with mental needles,
Twisting a mind as schoolboys twist a forearm,
Pinning a human fly beneath the tumbler.

Some of us populate our days and nights with
Enemies laying plots to trip or maim us,
To make us halt by roofs when tiles are falling
Or lose umbrellas, chances, buses, lovers.

Some of us wander reaching, reaching, reaching
Backwards in time as down into dark water
To find the clockwork mouse that broke, the woolly
Bear that we lost among the tall black fir-trees.

We are the dwellers in the middle limbo,
Land that we hate yet land that holds our landmarks,
Land where we cannot rest yet stay unresting,
Land that we long to leave but fear to start from.

We are the walkers in eternal circles
To whom the circle's better than its breaking,
To whom unhappiness has long grown easier
Than happiness ; to whom this twilight's home.

A. S. J. Tessimond.

IFFLEY

Ay, amor
que se fué no vino !

RIVER, green river
past flag-reeds swaying
and green paths of water
under the leaning rotten tree
river desiring the sea
you will reach where you are going.

Island, green island
with four poplars growing
when shall a way be found
past the rotten wooden fence,
island, to your innocence,
where the green light is playing ?

Tower, grey tower
over the past rising
your grey walls wail not for
the bones, the rotten lovers,
Towered once too to the stars,
beautiful, and died of their refusing.

O tower, island, river
O grey-green shore
all this shall have passed
like love, and turned rotten at last.

David Luke.

HARVEST

GLARING sun and stuffy air ;
Heat haze like river flowing.

This is good hiding grass
At the edge of the cornfield.
I lie right down
And no one can see me.

Stooks of corn like tiny fawn tents
Stand all over the field.
Men are forking the corn on to a cart.

I like having a ride on the gambo,
All bumpety-tumpety hard,
Like riding a train over the wheels
But much worse.
' Go on, Tom!
You are too slow for me,
I want you to gallop fast.'

I like riding on old Tom's bare back,
Soft and silky, and greasy with sweat.
When I hold his stringy mane
The muscles of his neck twitch
And his head bumps my hand
While his back goes smoothly along.

I've built a little house in the hedge,
A house with trees and logs,
Cool from the sun.

I watch the forking,
The cleaning of the field.
The crackly pale stubble
Pricks out of the ground
Of an empty cornfield.
Old Tom drags and pulls the gambo,
Tippling and wobbling,
Like a haystack crawling.
The last load!

Gillian Hughes.
(Aet. 7.)

SANTORIN[1]

Stoop if you can to the dark sea forgetting
The sound of a flute on naked feet
Stepping on your sleep in the other the sunken life.

Write if you can on your last shell
The day the name the land
And fling it in the sea that it may sink.

We stood naked on pumice-stone
Watching the islands rising,
Watching the red islands sinking
In their sleep in our own sleep
Standing naked here
We held the scales that were falling
In favour of Wrong.

Instep of power, unshadowed will, disciplined love
Plans that ripen in noontide sun
Avenue of Fate with the clapping of a new hand
On the shoulder ;
In a land that crumbled enduring no longer
In a land that once we possessed
The islands are sinking ashes and rust.

Ruined altars
The friends forgotten
Palm-leaves in mud.

Allow your hands to travel if you can
Here on the curve of time with the ship
That touched the horizon.
When the dice struck on the slab
When the lance struck on armour

[1] Santorin is geologically composed of pumice-stone and china-clay; in her bay...
islands have appeared and disappeared. This island was once the birthplace of a
very ancient religion. The lyrical dances of a strict and heavy rhythm performed
here were called Γυμνοπαιδίαι (*The Guide to Greece*).

When the eye discovered the stranger
And love grew dry
In pierced souls ;
When looking around you see
Feet reaped in a circle
Hands dead in a circle
Eyes dark in a circle ;
When there is no choice any longer
Of a death which you seek for your own,
Listening to a yell
Even the yell of the wolf
Your own justice ;
Allow your hands to travel if you can
Unfasten from treacherous time
Let yourself sink,

Must sink who carries the great stones.

George Seferis.
(*Translated from the Greek by* NANOS VALAORITIS.)

LAMENT

I

THE fury this Friday burst through my wall
    With a death certificate in its hand.
Bright, bright, Elipsion, burn to-night
    Across the sky and tell the whole
Empty and insignificant world that I grieve
    For a tall Jack with the sun on his wrist
And a sky stuffed up his sleeve. Let me leave
    Love on the mantelpiece looking East
To gather together the dust that I have lost.

II

They walk in silence over the same spaces
      Where they once talked, and now do not,
The dumb friends with the white-washed faces
      Who lifted a hand and died. They forget us
In the merciful amnesia of their death,
      But by us, the disremembered, they cannot
Ever be forgotten ; for always, in all places,
      They can rise eloquently up to remind us
Of the inalienable allegiances behind us.

III

My love, my love, why do you leave me alone ?
      My love, my love, where, where are you gone ?
Here the tall altitudes grieve as they gaze down
      Knowing that you, elusive their lover, are gone
      And that you will never again
Kiss the hands of the morning at a vivid four hundred,
      Uncurling, at nine angels, the splendid
Wake upon which you walk gold across the sky.
Grieving, like them, I cannot believe it is ended.

IV

Remember the eye that haunts me for ever
      Wherever I am, under any sky,
O completely from leaf and smiling from over
      Every horizon he looks at me.
The simple sea shall fold its sad arms
      Less long about the world
Than I shall hold him in my dreams
      Until every instant seems
      To reclaim part of him.

V

Here by the salt tide at the South
      That washes its coils along

The coast that lies behind the eyes,
      His wreck is like a rock in my mouth
With his body on my tongue.
      The salt that at the lashes of
All Seven Seas laces the shores,
      Grazing my weeping eye of sores,
Engenders the more of Love.

VI

Time with its shoving shall unsmooth
      The brightest lying lover
And in the teeth of human truth
Prove that the heart needs more than faith
      To help it to recover
The love that took a look at death
      And promised me for ever :
As, under Northern seas, his face
      Fades as the seas wash over.

VII

My love, my love, lift up your joystick hand,
      Dismiss the dividing
Grief. Bring, bring again the kiss and the guiding
      Glory. From his hiding
Place in the cleft of the cloud, O dove of evening,
Lead him back over that dark, that intervening
Day when he died, lead him back in a loving
      Return to this room where I
Look out and see his death glittering in the sky.

VIII

The killers shall spring into each other's arms
      And, sighing, the hate subside ;
The catalytical shall kiss, and the relief
Wrap cities in mutual belief,

And the dove preside.
And all but this tall one and the dead
Shall feel the warming of the world
Running through every board and bed
     Colder because they died.

IX

Sleep, long and beautiful, in that bag
     Where loneliness, my tall falcon,
Will never again cheat you with the mirage
     Of sensual satisfaction.
Look, look, the grave shakes over his head
     And the red dirt stands up, as
Across existence I beg him heed :
     To those that love there are no dead,
     Only the long sleepers.

George Barker.

THE AGE OF BLUE MEMORY

OLIVE-TREES and vines spreading to the sea,
And, beyond, red fishing-boats as far as memory,
The golden sheaths of August over our midday sleep
Full of sea-weed and shells. And this a green vessel
Newly built spelling in the waters' peaceful embrace :
     Our Lord will provide.

Like leaves, like pebbles the years went by,
I remember the young sailors leaving
With sails the colour of their hearts
They sang of the four horizons
They carried North winds tattooed on their chests.

What was I looking for when you came in the colour of dawn ?
The age of the sea in your eyes

The health of the sun in your body
—What was I looking for
Deep in the sea-caves in those spacious dreams
Where the wind flung his feelings like foam,
A blue stranger carving his sea-emblem on my chest.

With sand on my fingers I clasped my fingers
With sand on my eyes I clasped my fingers
It was the sadness
I remember it was in April when I first felt your human heaviness
Your human body of clay and sin
As on our first day on earth
The amaryllis were being celebrated—I remember
You suffered from a deep bite on the lips
A deep nail-mark on the skin
Where Time is being eternally traced.

I left you then

The wind thundered and swept the white houses
And scattered the clean white feelings over the sky
The light shining from a smile.

Now I shall have by my side a jug of immortal water
A form of the wind's shattering freedom
And these your hands where love suffers
And this your shell where echoes the Aegean.

Odysseus Elytis.

(*Translated from the Greek by* NANOS VALAORITIS.)

ELEGY

Do not expect, bewildered by your tears,
An easy answer for the heart or mind,
Nor sudden truth to blaze from the unseen,

Nor magic respite from the wound that sears ;
To die, that's certain, is to go behind
A wall no eye can pierce, however keen,
A curtain whose divide no hand shall find.

Millions have trusted what the legends tell :
The dead live on, their spirits freed from cares
Beyond our time and skies their praises sing
Throned in pure light or deep in asphodel ;
But never witness has returned, who bears
One trophy blossom from that deathless spring,
One sublime phrase of those Elysian airs.

The dead live on : but not in fields of bliss
Where the warm cheek we pressed shall lean again
Welcome to ours beneath the golden bough,
And every sorrow vanish in that kiss,
And not with angels, but in the living vein
Of all who sow behind their spirit's plough
And reap in cycles the maturing grain ;

And though the tears we shed will bring no smile
To lips once set in cold nobility,
It is love's wisdom so to weep, for grief
Can turn the hour of loss from cloudy ill
To that clear element where memory
Throbs like a sun that quickens earth to leaf,—
Their simple, mortal immortality.

Only the stabbing moment starts the cry :
' O loved one, whose last words vibrate like bells
Heard over water, you need have no fears,
All shall be done as if you were still by,
All change eschewed ' ; but the long grief compels
No dedication that may waste our years
Knowing no ghost in watchful silence dwells.

No ghost shall murmur comfort; therefore, though
If the raw wound should fester it would seem
Past bearing that one journey never will
Reach harbour where twin hopes had planned to go.
Love's elder faith may cleanse it and redeem
What is no more from nothing, so it still
Transforms the substance of each act and dream.

O miracles of grief we dare to know:
Down the long vista where the seagulls cry
Is it the promise of the fires of May
Over the green-starred branch-tips pulses so,
The April sun that laps caressingly,
Or the still purely blessing spirit's ray
Of one who loved too perfectly to die?

John Lehmann.

WAR

No, it is not these puffs of white
That burst above the forest's edge,
Suddenly on the sky's blue ledge
And slowly drift and thin from sight;

No, it is not the blows of shells
Like giant axes that behead
The firs, and stretch them out for dead,
The booming of these great steel bells;

No, it is not these sounds that tease
Among the fields of ripening grain,—
The whistling in the air again
The drone like giant swarms of bees;

It is this face behind my face
Close in the narrow trench we share,
The eyes I meet, their haggard stare
Stretched wide with horror of this place,

It is the solemn fixity
Emaciating mouth and nose,
The look, austere, resigned, of those
Whom death is calling silently;

It is for me, just round my lips
In the dank hole I've made my lair,
The rim of foam, if no one's there
I wipe off with my finger-tips.

André Chamson.

(*Translated from the French by* JOHN LEHMANN.)

CASTEL DI SANGRO

THERE was a sound of hunting in the mountains,
That came back dark and dangerous to the ears
Of those who crouched among the broken fountains:

The wounded wirecutter with his biting shears,
The trembling captain with his telephone,
The corporal with the ten-cent photos of his dears.

They all were lost and each one was alone,
Their uniforms were merely a disguise
That kept the naked earth from knowing naked bone.

' Shellshock—no visitors,' said the captain's eyes.
He was, himself, an isolation ward;
The sun and air and scenery were lies,

And if one wanted truth one had to guard
Oneself from all realities like men,
Yet men were always present. Truth came hard,

Especially when time and time again
The same huge shell exploded in his head,
And arms of strangers opened and, embracing, took him in.

The telephone he carried had been dead
For many hours—ever since They found
His battery with a salvo and had dyed the casings red.

It was dissolved from any further sound—
Mechanical foetus, with a broken cord
From which the wires jutted like bone chips in a wound.

The captain shivered, crouched, and spoke no word
To those beside him. His blue eyes were glazed;
And had he spoken they would not have heard.

For they, who once had looked, condemned, or praised,
Were caught up in the earthquake of the age,
Saw mount and man gape wide, and were amazed.

The wirecutter's wound was like a page
In some red book the world would always read,
It made him feel half pity and half rage.

Pity—that he'd been wounded and could bleed,
Rage—that the wounded statues had not bled,
Half-formed, he felt the marble's *having* and his need.

Beside him lay a smashed Apollo's head
He kicked it, and it rolled from him and caught
Against a cart whose occupants had fled.

Which was the living world, and which was not?
Upon the cold, cracked face there was a leer.
It was too high a price, but safety has been bought.

Immobile, lost between the far and near,
The corporal stared. A picture of his wife
And children was the object of a fear

That made him clutch the coppers of his life,
And dimmed his eyes and covered them with water,
And burned his vitals like a kiss or knife.

He studied the pale face of his one daughter
And then the smiling face of his one son :
These images had led him through the country of the mortar.

What had been done was done and would stay done.
He tucked the pictures in his helmet, grinning ;
Whatever the outcome of the war, he'd won.

The captain was the one who was not winning ;
He felt more war than went on in the town,
For him a peace would never be beginning.

Far from a lake or sea a man can drown,
Or smother in a universe of air.
Among the hosts of earth he weeps alone.

And thus these finally rose beneath the glare
And moved, automatons, beyond their night,
Doomed, yet unmastered, towards the waiting Stair,

And so they came, each one, into the light,
Among the shattered statues and the fountains' drouth,
Sun struck the broken columns for its own delight.

Their words had all gone silent in the mouth,
Their feet had all grown weary in the race,
The needle of the compass at last was pointing south.

And each one with a century in his face,
Turned and strode from the elemental guns,
Through streets whose rubble was a marble lace,

And through pellucid dust that met the sun's
Acclaiming rays traced the sullen war's
Sign on the suicide corporal and the other ones . . .

Dust on the corporal's stripes, the captain's bars,
Dust on the wounded wirecutter's gauze,
And dust that sifted towards the unseen, unmoved stars.

Harry Brown.
(U.S.A.)

THE ROAD TO NIJMEGEN

DECEMBER, my dear, on the road to Nijmegen,
between the stones and the bitter skies was your face.

At first only the gathering of graves
along the lank canals, each with a frosted
billy-tin for motto ; the bones of tanks
beside the stoven bridges ; old men in a mist
knifing chips from a boulevard of stumps ;
or women riding into the wind on the rims of their cycles,
like tattered sailboats tossing over the cobbles.

These at first and the fangs of homes, but more
the clusters of children like flies at the back of mess-huts,
or groping in gravel for knobs of coal,
their legs standing like dead stems out of their clogs.

Numbed on the long road to mangled Nijmegen,
I thought that only the living of others assures us ;
we remember the gentle and true as trees walking
as the men and women whose breath is a garment about us ;
that we who are stretched now in this tomb of time
may remount like Lazarus into the light of kindness
by a treasured hold in the hands of the kind.

And so in the sleet as we neared Nijmegen
searching my heart for the hope of our minds,
for the proof in the flesh of the words we miss,
for laughter outrising at last the rockets
I saw the rainbow answer of you,

of you and your seed who, peopling the earth, would distil
our not impossible dreamed horizon,
and who, moving within the nightmare Now
give us what creed we have for our daily crimes,
for this road that arrives at no future,
for this guilt
in the griefs of the old and the graves of the young.

Earle Birney.
(Canada.)

THE NIGHTMARE

THE nightmare was more vivid than the day—
I had escaped, I dared to hope again,—
The nightmare was a house that could not smile
For all its grey-winged eaves and trellis-rose,
The doves, the peacocks, everything was vain
In that secret base of souls who'd lost their way,—
But I had escaped, and climbed across the stile
Following the path that wound over the plain
Through fields so full of corn, the corn so ripe
In throbbing Summer's trance—O my blood froze
To hear them snigger at their victim's pain
And shoot again, and laugh, and calmly wipe
Blood from their boots, those souls where devils danced,—
But I had escaped, and somewhere in that plain
Knew there was a farm where love would rescue me
Welcoming with guiltless hand as he advanced,—
And there were giant statues black as jet

Prone at my feet, and in the ripened grain
Circles of ancient stones I paled to see
That hummed and rocked—and mysteries I forget.

The nightmare seemed as urgent when awake
As when I dreamed ; and though we ease our minds
As we might search an ebb-tide-cluttered shore
Tracing each image in the dire event
To drifting sea-wrack of the day before,
And in this flotsam soon elucidate
The patched disguise our exiled cravings take
To trick the coastguards ; yet such easing blinds
The searching eye that still may intimate
Some deeper riddle in the dream was meant,
And in those broken reels of drama finds
The symbol of the unapparent fate,
The act we dread but waits not our consent.

John Lehmann.

GREECE 1945

ALWAYS there was singing in this house,
The lights shining in the lemon tree outside :
And at night only the sound of the sea to be heard
When the leaves and stars had drunk the music in.
Then sleep closed peacefully under the green tiles,
Blessed by the full moon—until morning ruffled
The curtains and the children stirred.
I had never been beyond the mountains to the lands
Where the silks came from and the coloured birds.
There were sheep in this valley and wine
Tasting of the earth, the men busy all day
In the square fields, hearing the goat-bells
Play among the rocks ; and the baskets were full of fruit.
At carnival times I wore a mask and threw flowers ;

And I remember the laughter of the bearded priest,
Rough in the soft room, but how gentle his hands were
When children touched them. And there was singing,
Mostly of the old days, the songs like mottled marble
Enduring the long silence that is time.

Now returning to this valley I see the rubble and dust,
The charred beams where the laughter and singing was,
Where the music was before they came from the mountains,
The silk puffs of their guns exploding among the houses
And the green planes shouting at the sun.
I remember the tanks stumbling into the gardens
And the limp hands of the priest under the gibbet,
Leaves crinkling in the flame, smoke drifting over the water,
The goats frightened, the sheep stampeding to the hills.
That, too, was a long time ago and now I am afraid
Of the moonlight's mask upon men's faces
And of the wine spilled on bare floors.
I am afraid of the murdering sound of the sea.

Now I would wish to break from this valley for ever,
Where no ikons burn in altars along the roadside
And only the candles for the dead remain alight.
And the columns stand sentinels to the past
I cannot enter nor ever entirely lose.
I have nothing to offer but the images of terror,
The memories of too much suffering clouding the valley ;
And the bitter knowledge that only this hour matters
That we hold in our hands now, spilling over us like sunlight
On the sea there, brittle splinters of silver
Splashing our sorrow with momentary smiles :
Until darkness comes and the mystery of moonlight
And the sinister voices of the night wind,
Frogs croaking in the marshes, the stars mocking
The last stones of this temple where we stand.

H. B. Mallalieu.